History
of
Mexico

Iñigo Fernández

History of Mexico

◆

*A journey from
prehistoric times
to the present day*

MONCLEM
EDICIONES

HISTORY OF MEXICO
Translated by David Castledine
First edition: 2002
Sixth reprint: 2007
Copyright © by Monclem Ediciones, S.A. de C.V.
Leibnitz 31, Col. Anzures 11590 México, D.F.
monclem@monclem.com
Tel.: 52 55 47 67
Printed in Mexico
Impreso en México
ISBN 970-9019-12-0

Table of Contents

Introduction

It is often said that the wealth of a country is to be found in its history and culture. In this sense, Mexico is a fortunate nation as it does not lack either of these ingredients, on the contrary, it possesses a varied and interesting history which has enabled us who live in this country to inherit a very rich culture.

To understand Mexican history it is necessary to understand that Mexico is neither indigenous nor Spanish or, to put it differently, Mexico is the product of a fusion of these two cultures; a product which not only inherited "paternal and maternal" elements, but was also able to develop its own in the course of the centuries to acquire a personal stamp as a nation.

Although Mexico belongs to the great cultural and linguistic group of nations known as Latin America, its history is different from that of the rest, for while most of them shared the same liberators or insurgents during their wars of independence, Mexico had its own. While the rest of Latin American nations succeeded in winning independence without suffering great losses among their populations, Mexico had to lose a sixth of its inhabitants to achieve liberty. Mexico was the first Latin American country (and the first in the world) to carry out a revolution that was social in character in the early 20th century whose result was the promulgation of what was at the time the most advanced Constitution on earth.

For all the reasons stated above, readers have a synopsis of Mexico's past in their hands which retrieves the most important elements of it, those factors which have made this country what it is today.

Chapter 1

From man's arrival in America to the Aztec Empire 35,000 B.C. to 1519

Man reaches America

Among those who study prehistory the idea is upheld that the first settlers in America were not natives of the continent. Where did the first settlers come from? How did they reach America? There are two theories which attempt to answer these queries.

1.- A single origin. According to this, American man came from Asia. At the time of the last ice age sea levels fell and new land was temporarily exposed. This enabled Asians to cross the Bering Strait and settle in Alaska 35,000 years ago. The migrants continued on their way southwards in search of better lands and warmer climates favorable for hunting and later, gathering.

2.- Multiple origin. Those who uphold this theory recognize that although the Bering Strait was the most important migration route, it was not the only one. They affirm that Australasians and Malayo-Polynesians reached the continent thanks to their canoes and knowledge of sea currents and winds. Some physical and linguistic similarities among various ethnic groups of the north, center and south of the American continent support this hypothesis.

The first inhabitants of Mexico settled in the north of the country 20,000 years ago, but as they depended on hunting, they began to move

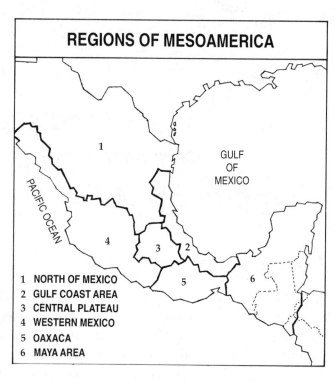

In the region of Mesoamerica, which covered Mexico, Guatemala and part of Honduras and El Salvador, some remarkable cultures flourished.

REGIONS OF MESOAMERICA

GULF OF MEXICO

PACIFIC OCEAN

1   **NORTH OF MEXICO**
2   **GULF COAST AREA**
3   **CENTRAL PLATEAU**
4   **WESTERN MEXICO**
5   **OAXACA**
6   **MAYA AREA**

south and concentrate in the Valley of Mexico because of its climate and the abundance of natural resources. This situation robbed them of their independence since once there was nothing left to hunt they had to journey to other regions to be able to survive. This way of life changed radically in the 7th century BC, when the Americans discovered agriculture, domesticating the corn plant. From that time forward, clans became sedentary and the first permanent settlements arose; a sex-based division of labor grew up, in which women devoted themselves to sowing and harvesting and the men to hunting. In short, agriculture led to the beginning of cultural development among certain American tribes.

Although all the territory of what is now Mexico was inhabited, only in certain areas of Mesoamerica was there a variety of cultural development. This region stretched far and wide: in the north it included what are now the states of Coahuila, Durango, Nuevo León San Luis Potosí, Sonora and Zacatecas, while to the south it reached the borders of what is now known as Nicaragua. In the course of 400 years, cultures grew in Mesoamerica that in spite of distances in time and space shared spiritual traits (the same gods under different names, the belief in life after death and the need to build temples to worship their deities) and material ones (agriculture, the use of lunar and solar calendars, specialized markets and stone carving).

For the study of Mesoamerican cultures, experts have grouped them into three periods or cultural horizons according to their age:

- The pre-Classic (2300 B.C. to 0).
- The Classic (0 to 900 A.D.)
- The post-Classic (900 to 1519 A.D.)

Several pre-Hispanic civilizations arose during these three periods: Olmecs, the cultures of the West, the cultures of the Central High Plateau, Totonacs, Huastecs, Zapotecs, Mixtecs, Mayas (who in turn divided into several subgroups), Tarascans, Toltecs, Teotihuacans, Tlaxcaltecs, Mexicas (Aztecs) Xochimilcans, Cholultecans, etc. Although each one of these groups was important in the region, only the ones whose political, economic, cultural and religious contributions had a powerful influence and brought about notable changes will be mentioned here.

The Olmec Culture

This was the first culture to emerge in Mesoamerica, in the pre-Classic era. Many historians have also given it the title of "mother culture" because it exerted its influence on other areas, such as the Central Plateau, Guatemala and El Salvador. Olmec groups settled in the states of Tabasco and Veracruz, in a hot region with plentiful fertile land bathed by the Grijalva and Papaloapan rivers.

Because it was the first culture in Mesoamerica, located in a very wet region, there are few material traces of the Olmecs and consequently little is known about them. Their language is completely unknown, and in fact the word "Olmec" is of Nahua origin and means "inhabitant of the rubber country." Due to the wetness, no human remains have been found that would tell us exactly what the Olmecs were like physically, but because of artistic representations such as monumental stone heads they are believed to have been short and thickset, with high cheekbones, crossed eyes, flattened noses and fleshy lips.

It is thought that there was no political union among them, since the system of city-states was the dominant one. Each one of these was a political, religious and economic center independent from the others, although they are believed to have kept close contact with one another. The most important urban centers were La Venta, Tres Zapotes and San Lorenzo

In each city-state there was a marked division of society. The priests had become the ruling class because of the religious, technical, mathematical, agricultural and writing knowledge they possessed. It is also believed that warriors belonged to the ruling class since their services in protecting cities and commercial activity, so important in the Olmec world, were very valuable. The rest of society was composed of craftsmen and farmers whose duty was to maintain the ruling class and the population as a whole.

Agriculture was the pillar of their economy. Using the system of *humedad y roza* (cutting down part of the vegetation and using the land for crops) they grew squash, chili, beans and corn (maize) in such quantities that they took advantage of the surplus produce to begin trading with different cultures. Olmec commerce evolved, passing from the exchange of food for raw materials that did not exist in "the rubber region" (stone, for example) to buying these, processing them and trading the finished product. There are two theories about the people involved in this activity. The first maintains that the warriors and priests undertook it, and the second suggests the existence of a group specialized in trade.

The Olmecs represented their deities with zoomorphic, anthropomorphic and mixed figures. Their gods were associated with the forces of nature, and the jaguar was the most important animal because of its strong symbolical charge. They connected it with death, water, fertility and agriculture; in other words, to the lifecycle.

The disappearance of the Olmecs is another mystery. Around 100 AD they vanished and nothing was ever known of them again. What is believed to have happened is that they scattered into the rain forest and ended by integrating with other groups, although what made them do so is not known.

The Teotihuacan Culture

One of the political, religious and trading centers that existed in the Classic cultural horizon was Teotihuacan. This urban center, whose name in Nahuatl means "the place where the gods live," lay east of Lake Texcoco and was founded by inhabitants from the Valley of Mexico around 300 BC. However, it was in the 7th century AD that the city reached its splendor, as an area covering a little over 20 square kilometers contained 100,000 inhabitants and its influence stretched through the present-day states of Hidalgo, Mexico, Morelos, Puebla and Veracruz.

Teotihuacan was the first city in Mesoamerica to have a theocratic and military government in which priests also carried out military duties. This group took decisions and controlled everything connected with trade; such was their importance that their dwellings were in the center of the city, which is now the archaeological site. The rest of society was composed mainly of craftsmen (there were almost no farmers) who constantly grew in numbers because of the city's commercial needs. Because of the need for this type of labor, immigrants from other areas, particularly Oaxaca, settled in Teotihuacan and created their own neighborhoods.

Disk from Chinkultic,
Chiapas showing
a ballgame player.

The principal, if not only, commercial activity was trade. They bartered knives, masks, spear points, blades —made of jade or obsidian — for food, stone and luxury products such as pectorals, bracelets, necklaces, amber and other sophisticated items. This commercial activity was so vigorous that Teotihuacan-made products reached such distant regions as those inhabited by the Mayas.

Religion was one of the major inheritances left by Teotihuacan to Mesoamerica. Many of the gods that emerged in this culture continued to be worshiped right up until the Spanish Conquest. Deities began to be shown with human bodies and those most venerated were Huehuetéotl, the god of fire and old age; the famous Tláloc, god of water; Yacatecuhtli, god of merchants, and Mictlantecuhtli, the god of death. The important religious ceremonies were held in the temples standing in the city center, and the rituals carried out there ranged from the chanting of hymns to human sacrifice.

The decline of Teotihuacan began between the 4th and 5th centuries and many factors go toward explaining this. The city grew so much that it damaged the environment and changed the climate: what had once been a fertile wooded region became a desert. The signs of destruction which appear in the ruins now lead to the belief that the city suffered outbreaks of violence which could have originated for various reasons: conflicts among the different ethnic groups living in the city, struggles between the ordinary people and the ruling class which had exploited them for centuries, or else invasions by Chichimecs (nomads from the north of the country) who set fire to the city on entering it. This culture fell into decline so rapidly and bloodily that by the 9th century it had become a ghost town.

The Maya Culture

The Mayas, groups which spoke different languages belonging to the same stock, covered a vast area that included what are now the states of Campeche, Chiapas, Quintana Roo, Tabasco and Yucatán as well as Belize, El Salvador, Guatemala and Honduras. In the Classic period, this area saw the emergence of important political, religious and social centers such as Bonampak, Copán and Palenque.

Politically speaking, the Mayas, just like the Olmecs, formed independent cities with a governor responsible for making any important decisions of an administrative, military, religious or legal nature. Although he had absolute power, a governor was accompanied by a council of elders who assisted him in administering the State and collecting taxes. At the same time, this council relied on other individuals in fulfilling their duties. And this was how the Mayas were able to build up a well-structured, functional system of administration.

Maya society was organized under a complex system. Each city had a ruling group of nobles who carried out administrative, intellectual and military duties, but collecting taxes from the population was one of their most important tasks. When the governor of a city died, the members of this group would meet to elect his successor from among them, although dynastic succession also existed. On a lower level were merchants who, although belonging to the inferior classes, lived well and luxuriously because their services were richly rewarded by the ruling elite who they supplied with luxury goods in abundance. On the lowest level were artisans and farmers, who were obliged to pay tributes in order to be free, have rights and be protected by the group in power. There were three reasons why people could become slaves: punishment, war, and by their own free will to pay off a personal debt.

The Mayas used the slash and burn technique and rain dependent land, taking advantage of the rainy season to grow corn, beans, squash, *jícama* yucca, sweet potatoes and cacao, the last of which was used exclusively for trading. With the passing of time, commerce grew to be the main economic activity. In local markets or by sending merchants to the Central Plateau and Central America the Mayas created a wide network which enabled them to exchange among themselves and with other peoples cacao, jade, honey, salt, fish, stone, amber, wood, quetzal feathers and deer and jaguar skins.

This culture was the one to show most interest in science and writing. Although they inherited the vigesimal system from the Olmecs, they refined it by introducing the concept of —and symbol for— zero. In astronomy, they invented the calendar of 365 days and the leap year, worked out the movements of Venus and could also predict when natural phenomena such as eclipses would occur. Measuring and registering time were activities that fascinated the Mayas who, not satisfied with having two calendars (solar, of 365 days, and lunar, of 260) created various units to record time which went from the *kin* (one day) to the *alautun* (64 million years).

In the arts, the Mayas were outstanding. Their imposing buildings topped with fine crests, their sculptures, pottery and paintings are all examples of this.

The Maya pantheon was made up of a series of gods which they related to the forces of nature, with daily life and such abstract concepts as numbers and months. The religious curiosity of these people led them to ask themselves questions about their origins and they came to the conclusion that before them, others had existed who, because of their religious and physical deficiencies, had been destroyed by the gods. The most venerated deities were Itzamná, the supreme god:

Kukulkán, god of wind; Yum Kaax, god of corn; Chaac, god of water; Yum Kimil, god of death, and Kinich Ahau, god of the sun and time, among others.

Between the beginning of the 10th century and halfway through it the great Maya centers started to be abandoned by their inhabitants. This is believed to have been the consequence of soil exhaustion, population growth, civil wars, natural disasters and invasions by other tribes.

The Toltec Culture

The fall of Teotihuacan, together with the decline of the Maya culture are the events that marked the transition to the post-Classic period. In this epoch, Mesoamerica suffered a succession of Chichimec invasions which brought about a series of changes in the region.

One of the first Chichimec groups to settle in Mesoamerica were the Toltecs. These outstanding "pupils" of the Teotihuacans, the Toltecs founded the city of Tollán (Tula), which in the course of time would become the capital of a vast empire. It was in the region of the High Central Plateau that the Toltecs first exercised their hegemony, but not content with this they took up arms to widen their area of influence, finally controlling such distant regions as Guerrero, Oaxaca and Yucatán.

Among the Toltec rulers there was one who stood out for his civilizing spirit and not so much for the love of weapons. Topiltzin wanted Tollán to become a center of culture and to make this dream come true he encouraged craftsmen and architects from the Valley of Mexico to go and settle there. This change also had an important religious repercussion, as the king gave great impulse to the cult of Quetzalcóatl (feathered serpent), a peace-loving god closely linked with culture, as opposed to Tezcatlipoca (smoking mirror), the god of war. This religious change may have been so radical that most of the Toltecs rose in arms and deposed Topiltzin.

Government of the Toltecs was in the hands of a group of priests who exerted an iron control over the rest of the population although —in contrast to earlier civilizations— this group was not coherent and its members were constantly quarreling, a situation which led to a civil war. It is believed that the farmers and merchants, the pillars of Toltec society and economy took no part in politics and consequently in any decision-making.

Trade and agriculture were the most important economic activities in the Toltec world. Although they had learned to sow and plant from the Teotihuacans, the Toltecs are thought to have preferred to obtain their food supplies from tribes that had to pay them tribute. At the same time, trade ranked high among them, with pottery and obsidian as their main goods.

Little is known about Toltec religion. They were the first to have war gods, such as Tezcatlipoca, the god of both night and war. Other important deities were Tláloc, the god of water, Quetzalcóatl, the god of dawn and wisdom: Tlazoltéotl, goddess of fertility and Centeocíhuatl, the goddess of corn.

The Toltec culture began to decline in the 12th century as a result of invasions by other Chichimec tribes, civil wars and uprisings by tribute-tribes. Most of the city's inhabitants deserted it to take refuge in the Valley of Mexico in the surroundings of the lake region where other Chichimec tribes had settled two centuries earlier.

The Mexica Culture

One of the Chichimec groups of Nahua origin who had taken part in the fall of Tollán was that of the Mexicas or Aztecs. Natives of a mythical city which they called Aztlán —supposed to be located in Nayarit— the Aztecs began to migrate toward the High Plateau in the year 1111 in search of better living conditions. When they reached the Valley of Mexico, the states established there (Azcapotzalco, Culhuacán and Xochimilco for example) were fully engaged in a process of expansion and war. After they had served the Tepanecas and Colhuas as mercenaries, in 1325 the king of Azcapotzalco granted them a small islet in the middle of Lake Texcoco for them to settle on. Immediately afterward, the Aztecs founded Mexico-Tenochtitlan, a simple city which had certain privileges such as different ecosystems and water all the time. In spite of adopting a sedentary lifestyle and enjoying these advantages, the Aztecs could neither hide nor control their warlike spirit and began to put a policy of expansion into practice that led them first to conquer their neighbors and later the Valley of Mexico itself and to extend their supremacy to Guerrero, Hidalgo, Morelos, Tlaxcala, Oaxaca, Puebla, Veracruz and Chiapas. When the Aztecs became a dominant power they decided to change their history and began to claim that the reason for their wanderings had originated in an order given to them by the god Huitzilopochtli. This deity, related to war, indicated to the Aztec priests that the exodus would end when they reached a place where an eagle was perched on a cactus, devouring a snake. According to legend, this place proved to be Mexico-Tenochtitlán.

The political system they governed themselves under was strict and perfectly ordered. At the head was the emperor (*tlatoani*), who was the supreme authority as far as religion, war and politics were concerned. When the emperor died, the nobles would meet to chose his successor from among themselves. Below him was the counselor (*cihuacóatl*), who performed various functions, which ranged from substituting for the emperor when he was absent, to taking charge of the collection and storage of tribute. He was followed by the State Council or Tlatocan which, apart from advising the emperor when he requested, was responsible for everyday administrative and legal matters.

The Aztecs had a strict education for young men of noble stock. They were sent to a school known as *calmecac*, where they learned the laws of honor, how to fight and discipline to withstand pain.

Society was divided into two estates. The *pipiltin* were the members of the nobility; they held the political, military and religious posts, did not pay taxes and were prohibited from doing any work connected with the land. The rest of society, the *macehualtin*, were responsible for

The ninth Aztec
ruler, Moctezuma
Xocoyotzin.

keeping the productive system alive; whether they were merchants, craftsmen, farmers, porters, soldiers or slaves...they all had to pay taxes if they wanted to enjoy political rights so restricted that they could only exercise them at the level of city neighborhoods (*calpulli*).

The economy underwent changes with time. At first, agriculture was the central element of it. Using the *chinampas* —the "floating gardens" which can still be seen today in Xochimilco— rotation of crops and terraces, peasants grew beans, corn, chili and squash in such vast quantities that the Aztecs usually had surpluses. As warfare gradually became a way of life, the Aztecs found that another way of enriching their economy was exacting extremely high tribute from the peoples they conquered. The amount of the tribute to be paid varied according to the wealth of the region subjugated. Trade was another extremely important economic activity in the Aztec world. In markets *(tianguis)* exchanges between producers and consumers was direct and was a well planned way for city dwellers to have different products at hand. There was long-distance trade, for which merchants *(pochteca)* walked or sailed thousands of kilometers to obtain the products esteemed by the *pipiltin.*

The principal, most feared gods of the Aztecs were Huitzilopochtli, the supreme warrior god and Coatlicue, goddess of fertility, the mother of Huitzilopochtli, in addition to Tláloc, Xochipilli, Ehécatl, Xipe Totec and others which made up the Aztec pantheon. Human sacrifices were a constant feature based on the belief that blood was the nourishment the sun needed to be able to rise every day, and this is why they fought wars against neighboring tribes to take prisoners for sacrifice.

There were eleven Aztec monarchs: Acamapichtli, Huitzilihuitl, Chimalpopoca, Izcóatl, Moctezuma Ilhuicamina. Axayácatl. Tizoc, Ahuitzotl, Moctezuma Xocoyotzin, Cuitláhuac and Cuauhtémoc. The last two fought against the Spaniards for the freedom of their people.

The Aztecs succeeded in raising the mightiest empire in the history of Mesoamerica, yet it was ephemeral if it is compared to other great cultures of the region. It was neither uprisings nor ethnic wars that led to this situation, nor did the exhaustion of natural resources or the traditional Chichimec invasions have anything to do with it. The cause was the sudden intrusion of a new force different from all those existing in Mesoamerica, a new power in which religious and economic motives were the driving forces and which was ready to destroy anything and everything that was different from it: Spain.

Chapter 2

The Conquest of Mexico and the Viceroyalty (1519-1808)

The Conquest and the first Governments (1492 - 1535)

It was thanks to the four voyages Columbus made between 1492 and 1502 that the gates of America were opened to the Spanish. In the belief that these new lands were a reward God had given them for expelling the Moors from their soil, hundreds of Spaniards emigrated to America with the illusion of becoming owners of great lands and fabulous treasures.

The first Spanish settlements in America grew up in the Caribbean, but the exhaustion of both natural and human resources, together with the constant arrival of immigrants, were factors that drove the Spanish to look for new lands and riches in the northwest of the continent.

The governor of Cuba, Diego Velázquez, was an ambitious man who realized that the more he promoted the search and conquest of new lands, the more his fame and wealth would increase considerably. In 1517 he organized the first Spanish expedition to what is today Mexico and placed at is head Francisco Hernández de Córdoba, an experienced soldier who had helped Velázquez in the conquest of Cuba. Things went well for the explorers in the first days of the voyage but when they reached the coast of Yucatán and tried to establish contact with the natives, these showed their aggressiveness and killed several Spaniards in fights. Hernández de Córdoba refused to give up and gave the order to continue following the coast as far as what is now Campeche. But the situation grew worse, since when the natives saw the Spaniards disembark they attacked them ferociously. Many were killed and others, including the captain of the mission, seriously wounded. After this reversal the expedition limped back to Cuba on a voyage that ended in 1518.

Although the journey had not been economically profitable, neither was it a complete failure because those who took part in it affirmed that they had found civilizations more culturally advanced than those in the Caribbean. Velázquez' ambition was increased by the thought that greater development meant greater riches; therefore, in that same year he organized a second expedition led by Juan de Grijalva, another veteran of the conquest of Cuba.

In spite of the reports he had received, Grijalva followed in the steps of the first expedition and although he also clashed with the Mayas, there were very few casualties. Passing Campeche, he continued sailing northwest until he reached Tabasco. There he decided to advance inland following the great mouth of a river. The natives of the region were more friendly than the Mayas of the coast and thanks to this the Spaniards were able to disembark several times and exchange glass beads for precious metals.

When the second expedition returned to Cuba, Juan de Grijalva was carrying booty worth 20,000 pesos and, what was more important, news about the existence of an immensely rich empire inland. This comment was enough to prompt the governor of the island to start organizing a fresh expedition.

By early 1519, Diego Velázquez had the third expedition ready, which was to be commanded by Hernán Cortés, a captain born in Extremadura in 1485, with 15 years of military experience in America. Despite the friendship between them, secretly Cortés did not share the excessive ambition of the governor, who even asked him to conquer the native lands, strip the inhabitants of all the gold they possessed and not to settle the new lands with Spaniards; this last request was against the wishes and orders of the Spanish Crown.

The conquistador
Hernán Cortés.

As time passed, Cortés could not continue pretending. Whenever he could, Velázquez made him understand that although he was captain of the expedition, he was his subordinate. Cortés began to complain about the constant humiliation he was subjected to, and his enemies on the island, who could not have been few, took advantage of this false step to persuade the governor to take the command of the expedition away from him. When Cortés heard about this move, he lost no time and brought the beginning of the enterprise forward. On February 18, 1519, without permission from Diego de Velázquez, Hernán Cortés embarked on the process which, though he did not know it, would end with the conquest of Mexico-Tenochtitlán.

Three days after sailing from Cuba the Spaniards reached the island of Cozumel (Yucatán) where they learned that Brother Jerónimo de Aguilar and Gonzalo Guerrero, Spanish survivors of a shipwreck in 1511, had integrated into the Maya community of the locality. Cortés invited them to join his expedition, but Guerrero did not accept because he had married a Maya woman and had several children by her.

However, Aguilar, who was a slave, joined the Spaniards and put his knowledge of the Maya language at their service.

Cortés and his men followed the routes pioneered by Hernández de Córdoba and Grijalva. When they reached Tabasco, they had some clashes with the Maya chieftains living there, but these, after being defeated —thanks to the horses, armor and firearms— they decided to make peace with the invaders, whom they honored with food, gold, cotton cloaks and young women. Among these women was one called Malinalli, also known as Malintzín, Malinche and Marina, who played an important role in the conquest due to her knowledge of both the Maya and Náhuatl languages. In this way, when Cortés wanted to ask the Indians about something, Aguilar translated the question into Maya and Malinalli from Maya into Náhuatl and later into Spanish, which she quickly learned.

The first contact between the Aztecs and the Spaniards took place a few days later, after the latter had founded the settlement of Santa María de la Victoria. The party sent by Moctezuma II, the ninth Aztec monarch, were left impressed when Cortés and his men put on a performance in which horses ran hither and thither while the soldiers fired volleys from their rifles and cannons. The envoys were amazed and confirmed the divine origin of the strangers —whom they named *teules* or gods— whose arrival coincided with the mythical date of return prophesied by the god Quetzalcóatl. Therefore, the ambassadors of Moctezuma, who at this moment was full of superstitious fears —laid substantial gifts at Cortés' feet (gold, jewels, cotton clothes) in the hope that his ambitions would be satisfied and he would retreat. The effect was quite the opposite, Cortés took this to be a small sample of the riches that existed in these lands and now was even more eager to press on inland to the capital of the Aztec empire.

Before continuing on the expedition, Cortés had to resolve a personal problem. Aware that he had broken the law by leaving Cuba without the governor's permission, who he depended on directly, he decided to give his actions legality to prevent Vázquez from taking steps against him. Together with his men, he founded Villa Rica de la Vera Cruz (now Veracuz) and before the council of the settlement renounced the power given to him by the governor of Cuba and assumed the title of Captain General and Chief Justice, by which he became directly answerable to the king of Spain, Charles I. Here, Cortés was faced by another delicate situation. Some of his men wanted to go back to Cuba and not continue marching inland. In reply to this, Cortés ordered the ships to be made useless to force everybody forward.

On the route to Mexico-Tenochtitlan, the Spaniards witnessed the abuse suffered by the peoples who paid the Aztecs tribute. When they arrived in Cempoala the chieftain —known as "the fat one" because of his obesity— gave them men, provisions and information on the region in exchange for military protection. This alliance showed Cortés that many tribes hated the Aztecs and that this could work in his favor if he forged alliances with the dissenters along his way.

The policy of alliances bore fruit, since as the Spaniards passed through Puebla, indigenous groups joined them, in the belief that they were gods. All this changed however when they reached Tlaxcala. This was a state which had managed to stay independent from the Aztecs, who in revenge had imposed a trade embargo on cotton, cacao and salt, in addition to fighting them to obtain prisoners for sacrifice in battles known as "Flowery Wars." Cortés sent envoys to agree on an alliance with them but Xicoténcatl, one of the most important Tlaxcaltec leaders, distrusted the Spaniards and prepared to wage war on them. After several defeats, the Tlaxcaltecs recognized the superiority of the Spanish troops and also saw in them a way to end Aztec domination. While the Spaniards were resting in Tlaxcala another suite arrived from Moctezuma with gifts and a message from the emperor asking Cortés to give up his idea of going to the capital of the empire. This suggestion was disregarded.

The Spaniards, reinforced with the incorporation of Tlaxcaltec troops, headed toward Cholula, an independent state which had good relations with the Aztecs. When they arrived the Cholultecs, by order of Moctezuma, gave them a warm welcome, something which caused suspicion among the Europeans and was used by the Tlaxcaltecs to make them believe it was a conspiracy. Cortés investigated whether there was such a plot, and having verified this ordered a brutal repression in which priests, warriors and a large part of the population were killed. The victims of this incident, which came to be known as the Cholula Massacre, are estimated to have been between four and five thousand.

After what happened in Cholula the Tlaxcaltecs guided the Spaniards to the Valley of Mexico between the volcanoes Iztaccíhuatl and Popocatépetl through what is known today as "the pass of Cortés" from where they were impressed by the magnificent prospect of Tenochtitlan. The chieftains of towns on the way offered their friendship to the Spaniards who, after passing through Amecameca, Chalco and Ixtapalapa finally reached Mexico-Tenochtitlan. It was November 8, 1519.

Cortés and Moctezuma met for the first time on the Xólotl ditch, at a point located on what is now Pino Suárez street near the later Hospital de Jesús. Cortés was impressed by the number of people who turned out and also by the size and splendor of the emperor's court. At the same time, Moctezuma was amazed by the color of the foreigners and the strange animals that accompanied them. The atmosphere during these first days was cordial; the Spaniards were accommodated in the palace of Axayácatl; every day they were taken through the city, while Cortés and Moctezuma spent nights talking about the history, religion and customs of their peoples. However, relations between the two began to cool as a result of two things. News arrived that the chieftain of Nautla had put several Spaniards to death; in answer, Cortés made Moctezuma, much against his will although the orders came from him, to punish his vassal with death. On another occasion, Cortés entered the Great Temple and began to destroy the statues of gods, considering them contrary to the Catholic faith. But all this ended when Cortés took Moctezuma prisoner in an attempt to avoid a possible Aztec uprising.

While this was happening in the Aztec capital, troops sent by Diego Velázquez and headed by Pánfilo de Narváez disembarked in Veracruz with the order to take Cortés prisoner and his captains to return them to Cuba. When Cortés heard about this he left Pedro de Alvarado in charge of Tenochtitlan and headed for Veracruz with some men to confront Narváez.. It was in Cempoala that the two Spanish armies met, with that of Cortés dominating. Narváez was apprehended and later sent to Cuba, while his arms and soldiers stayed in the hands of the victor.

Meanwhile, Pedro de Alvarado made the situation of the Spaniards in Mexico-Tenochtitlan worse because after having authorized the Aztecs to hold a religious festival in the Great Temple he appeared there and began a terrible attack that would pass into history as the "Great Temple Massacre". Anger swept through the native population; they armed themselves and went out into the streets to fight the Spaniards and Tlaxcaltecs, who were forced to take shelter in the palace of Axayácatl and began to suffer the effects of a cruel siege. This is why when Cortés arrived back in Tenochtitlan he found the streets empty and the few Aztecs he met were hostile to him. When he gained entry to the palace the conquistador was informed about the events that had caused the rebellion and, after pondering over this, came to the conclusion that the solution to the problem was to oblige Moctezuma to calm his subjects. The emperor walked out onto a balcony to face a turbulent crowd which, on seeing him, began to shout complaints against him and throw stones. According to the story, one of these rocks hit him on the head and caused his death, although it is also believed that he may have been murdered by Cortés himself. The Aztec nobles lost no time, but gathered and chose as the new emperor Cuitláhuac, a young warrior, who had the siege strengthened. Faced with this failure the Spaniards realized that the only choice left to them was to try to break through and retreat from the city. In the early hours of July 1, 1520 the Spaniards —who had already shared out the gold found in the palace of Axayácatl— and the Tlaxcaltecs left the building with the utmost caution. As they were advancing along the Tacuba causeway, the Aztecs became aware of the escape and began the pursuit. Hundreds of Spaniards, Tlaxcaltecs, cannons and horses were crowded together on the narrow causeway, from which the Aztecs had already removed the bridges. Numberless soldiers and horses were drowned, while almost all the artillery and treasure disappeared into the depths of Lake Texcoco. The survivors were able to rest when they reached Popotla, where Cortés is said to have leaned against a tree to weep bitterly over

Cuauhtémoc, the last
Aztec ruler.

the defeat suffered that night, known since then as the "Sad Night."
The Spaniards did not remain there but continued on to Tlaxcala to
recover and plan a counterattack, but at Otumba they were attacked
again by the Aztec army. In spite of his weakness in numbers, Cortés
was able to defeat the Aztecs.

Once in Tlaxcala, Cortés began to plan a new campaign against the
Aztecs, which was based on the idea of conquering all the territory
lying between this domain and Mexico-Tenochtitlan in a kind of cordon
that would be closed tighter as the conquistadors neared their target.
Meanwhile, in the Aztec capital, a smallpox epidemic had broken out,
probably carried by one of Narváez's men. Because this was a disease
unknown in the pre-Hispanic world large numbers of natives fell victim
to it, the most important being the young emperor Cuitláhuac. After
his death, the noble Cuauhtémoc took his place.

From late 1520 the Spaniards resorted to arms and alliances to
penetrate into the Valley of Mexico once again. Once there, Cortés began
to lay siege to the Aztec capital, and for many, this was nothing more
than his revenge for the humiliation of the "Sad Night." With the help

of the kingdoms adjoining Tenochtitlan the Spaniards blocked the exits of the causeways and used brigs (small ships fitted with cannons)) that had been built on Lake Texcoco to surround the Aztec capital. From this time on, not a single person could enter or leave the city without permission from the Spaniards. Not content with this Cortés had a section of the Chapultepec aqueduct broken to cut off the supply of drinking water (the lake water was brackish). Despite these adversities, the Aztecs stoically bore the siege and when the Spaniards and their thousands of Tlaxcaltec allies began to attack the city on August 13, 1521, they defended it ferociously. The battle between the two sides was merciless, according to both native and European accounts. On every street, hordes of Aztec, Spanish and Tlaxcaltec soldiers could be seen fighting and even when the latter won they were not able to advance far because a new contingent of natives would confront them. The battle ended when the Spaniards finally took Cuahtémoc prisoner. The story goes that when he saw he was deprived of his freedom he asked Cortés to kill him with a dagger, since he had done all he could to defend his people. The Spaniard ignored his words and for the moment, pardoned him his life. The siege of Tenochtitlan finished on August 13, 1521.

Many experts say that the conquest of Mexico-Tenochtitlan was the bloodiest and most devastating of all those the Spanish carried out in America. Of the formerly proud and majestic Indian capital there only remained piles of stones and smoldering wood, bodies and haggard faces. On the ruins of great Tenochtitlan the city that would be the capital of New Spain began to rise.

The first Governments (1521 - 1535)

After the Conquest Cortés had to confront problems deriving from it. The first was the question of government, an easy job on paper, but extremely thorny in practice. Ever since the creation of the town council *(ayuntamiento)* of Villa Rica de la Vera Cruz the conquistador had held the post of Captain General and Governor of New Spain, duties that were ratified by the Crown in 1522. Although Cortés had full power in the land, he chose his closest friends to fill the most delicate political and legal posts, so causing the enmity of the other conquistadors. When he considered he had established the bases of New Spain's government he lost no time but launched himself into new military enterprises for, as he himself said, he was "more of a doer than a bystander." He decided to undertake an expedition to Las Hibueras (Honduras) in 1524, an expedition that turned out a disaster and during which he had Cuauhtémoc, the last Aztec emperor, hanged. On his departure, a conflict broke out between his friends and his detractors, and the latter won power. They followed a policy of persecuting Cortés' friends. This led to two things: the return of Cortés to the capital of New Spain in 1526 and the Crown sending a judge who was to try Cortés and take over command in these lands. The judge, Alonso de Estrada, governed until 1529, when he was removed because he took sides in internal disputes.

Because of this situation King Charles I thought it wise to entrust the government of New Spain to an *Audiencia* in which its president and four judges would have absolute power. This move failed because the person at the head was Nuño de Guzmán, a corrupt and pitiless adventurer who lost no time in colluding with his companions and committing a series of abuses against both the Indians (an excessive increase in taxes) and the Spanish (stripping Cortés' followers of their *encomiendas* (native villages). This behavior was so disgraceful that the bishop of Mexico, Juan de Zumárraga, sent reports about what was happening in New Spain to Charles I. The king suspended this audiencia and replaced it with a second one in 1530. To avoid abuses he named men of proved integrity presidents and judges such as Brother Vasco de Quiroga. This *audiencia* worked for the Crown by imposing order in New Spain by annulling everything that had been done by the first *audiencia*, bringing the native population back to normality and carrying out a judicial review (applied to all the king's representatives who governed in America) of Nuño de Guzmán.

During his term of office as Captain General Cortés organized an expedition consisting of three ships. He reached Baja California,

The first viceroy,
Antonio de Mendoza.

exploring the sea which now bears his name. The conquistador died in Spain in 1547 and years later his remains were transferred to Mexico.

In five years, the Second Audiencia succeeded in imposing an order that had never been seen before in these lands. But in 1535 Charles I decided to make important political changes since he wished to install a form of government that would be more loyal to him than any other and which, at the same time, would control the Spaniards who, on the pretext of the distance, were showing too much independence. It was for these reasons that Charles decided to make New Spain a viceroyalty.

The Viceroyalty (1536 - 1700)

The king of Spain was the supreme ruler of New Spain, but as he could not travel to the country to govern it directly, he sent a representative to take measures in his name. This representative was known as the viceroy.

33

The viceroy of New Spain in theory held absolute power. Viceroys had five duties. As governors they had to ensure that the Indians were not maltreated; make appointments to low-level political posts; attend to matters concerning food, morals and health, and issue decrees. As captains general they had to take charge of pacifying the country, mainly in regions where the Indians were sedentary, and of defending it against possible attacks from outside. In their position as superintendents of the Royal Treasury they were responsible for the finances of the vice-royalty. As vice-patrons of the Church they had authorization to intervene in matters of both the regular and secular clergy, and also to supply parishes with priests proposed by the bishops.

The audiencia, composed of a president and four judges (*oidores*) governed together with the viceroy. This functioned as the main judicial authority in New Spain. By means of civil and criminal courts it administered justice, while with the court of appeal it could reverse sentences given by the viceroy, whom it advised on administrative and legal matters and who it could substitute for in his absence. The audiencia, in short, was created by the Spanish Crown to limit the viceroy's power and prevent him from committing excesses.

The most important cities were governed by *corregidores*, Spaniards appointed by the king for the task. *Alcaldes mayores* however, —who worked closely with the corregidores— were chosen by the viceroy and their job was to collect and administer taxes. Below them were the municipal councils (*ayuntamientos*), composed of Spanish inhabitants of the cities where these had been established. Within these were the cabildos or town councils made up of community mayors (*alcaldes menores*) and councilors (*regidores*). Who were responsible for applying the directives of the viceroyalty or resolving minor local problems. The municipal model was also applied to Indian communities, but with certain differences because Europeans (except priests and missionaries) were forbidden to enter them and the system of feudal domains controlled by caciques was allowed to remain. These chiefs were treated as nobles and given certain privileges, such as exemption from taxes.

As the territorial expansion of New Spain grew in the 16th, 17th and 18th centuries, the town councils acquired more importance, since they became the ways of maintaining Spanish political and economic control.

As mentioned earlier, questions of the discovery, conquest and colonization of lands in America are linked to the search for gold and silver. New Spain was no exception, for the economic doctrine in vogue in the 16th century was mercantilist, whose ruling principle was that the wealth of a country lay in the amount of precious metals it possessed. This, of course, did not run counter to the accumulation of lands as a means to generate wealth for individuals. This is why at this period there was a close relationship between the type of land ownership, the different forms of native labor and traditional economic activities (agriculture, stock raising, etc.)

The *encomienda* was the first type of land ownership that the Spaniards put into effect. Its origin is linked to the conquest of Mexico-Tenochtitlan itself, since when this was accomplished, the conquistadors realized that the spoils of war were scarce. They were very angry, and so before they could revolt, Cortés went against the orders of the Crown and began to give out encomiendas among them.

The holders of encomiendas —encomenderos— were not given ownership of the land and all that was in it, but the right to its usufruct, in exchange for which they swore to be loyal to the Crown and foster the conversion and education of the Indians —also called encomendados. In practice, this system was a failure because of the abuses committed by the encomenderos, who did not care about what the laws and the Crown demanded of them They kept a larger portion than they were due to of the tributes, demanded gold as tribute from the Indians, obliged them to stay off the land of their communities for more than twenty days and did nothing about their evangelization, all flagrant violations of the *Ordinancs of good government* issued by Cortés in 1524.

The Crown looked askance at this system since it was clear that the encomenderos were acquiring a lot of power and showed a growing independence from Spain. In 1542 the first viceroy, Antonio de Mendoza, by order of Emperor Charles V showed his mettle by signing a decree establishing that no more encomiendas were going to be handed out and that the grandchildren of the encomenderos would not inherit this privilege, since the encomiendas passed into the hands of the Crown.

At the beginning of the 17th century, the encomienda system was in decline thanks to the efforts of the Crown and the dramatic fall the Indian population saw due to abuses and sickness in the second half of the 16th century.

The encomienda was succeeded by the *repartimiento*. Under this system, all male Indians between the ages of 14 and 60 (with the exception of the nobles of each community) had to contribute labor to their Spanish employers. Every six months, communities sent gangs, and the work was not to last for more than two weeks. Indians were employed in agriculture, mining, public works and domestic service. In exchange workers received payment in proportion to the type of work done and the time spent on it. On each repartimiento there were royal officials to ensure that the Spanish employers did not abuse the Indians, although in fact this happened very often.

In the early 18th century the Crown suppressed the repartimientos as a result of pressure from the priests who protected the Indians, and the opinion that this was a matter of forced labor. Its place was taken by voluntary, paid work in which workers in the agricultural, industrial, stock raising and mining sectors made an agreement with their employers to receive wages for their efforts.

In another order of ideas, one of the effects produced by the Crown was the uniting of the Spanish and Mesoamerican production structures. New animals arrived (horses, cows, sheep, goats, chickens), work tools (wheels and mills) and crops (wheat, sugarcane and flax) which were combined with the products the Indians used (turkeys, beans, sisal hemp, corn, etc.).

The development of economic activities in New Spain was not anarchic or improvised; the Spanish Crown devised it in such a way as to satisfy its economic and commercial needs. It is not surprising, therefore, that inside the viceroyalty —like in the rest of Spanish

America— regional specialization in the production of goods and services should have arisen.

Initially, agriculture developed slowly as a result of the need to acclimatize crops brought from Europe and the Spaniards' lack of interest in doing this type of work themselves which, because it was manual, they considered beneath them. In the course of time however, the majority of the Spanish crops began to be grown in these lands and were adopted into the dietary habits of New Spain. Some crops however, such as grapevines and olives were prohibited by the Crown because they affected the merchants who shipped wine and olive oil from Spain and paid extremely high import duties.

The arrival of the Spanish brought about a far-reaching change in agriculture. They introduced crop rotation which gave the land more life and used its nutrients in a balanced way. They also increased the fertility of land by using animal manure and made sowing faster with the use of plows, wheels and teams of draft animals.

The Indians, those most affected by this agricultural revolution, were able to adapt very well to the changing times: on the one hand they continued to consume corn, beans, chili and maguey cactus, and on the other incorporated small amounts of wheat, sugarcane and linseed into their diet.

The interior regions of the Viceroyalty specialized in growing wheat, squash and barley, while coastal areas produced cacao, sugarcane, cotton, vanilla and indigo.

In contrast to agriculture, stock raising had no problems of growth in New Spain. The reasons for this are simple: in the Mesoamerican world there were no beasts of burden or draft animals, and in addition the geography and climate —great plains and temperate conditions— favored the development of stock raising in the country.

From the very beginning, horses were essential for the Spaniards because apart from being a status symbol, because of their cost, they were a vital means of transport to cover the immense distances of New Spain. In time, there were so many of these animals that even poor whites and mestizos could afford them.

Donkeys were important too. Brought from Spain, they were used as beasts of burden and draft animals, helping Indian porters —*tamemes*— to give up this exhausting task and devote themselves to other, less demanding, ones.

In addition to these animals, beef cattle, pigs, sheep and goats also proliferated. These animals were so readily accepted by the Indians that they reproduced rapidly. The eating habits of communities changed because goats, cattle, poultry and pigs became part of the native diet. Sheep were also welcomed, since thanks to them they began to wear woolen clothes.

The Spaniards devoted themselves to managing heavy livestock and made considerable amounts trading meat and hides. This type of livestock created problems: they often invaded the lands of indigenous communities, causing damage and conflicts between cattle raisers and the Indians. As cattle moved into the north of the country where there were vast stretches of land without native communities, the problem was resolved.

Without any doubt, mining was the most buoyant economic activity of New Spain and, consequently, of Spain. As the subsoil belonged to the Crown, it licensed it to individuals in the wish to encourage the exploitation of precious metals. Whoever acquired the mine had to pay the Crown the equivalent of one twentieth of its production every year and also pay a fifth of the value of every gold or silver ingot assayed and stamped by representatives of the Spanish government.

As New Spain expanded northward, mining increased. The arrival of the Spanish in the region of Guanajuato marked the beginning of growth in the mining industry of New Spain since, as used to be said in the 16th century, the region was so rich in silver that the veins could be seen on the ground. Despite this, mining had to face and resolve two problems: labor and how to purify silver.

While the central region was densely populated by Indians, in the north there were few, and therefore people were in short supply and in addition many died because of the arduous work in the mines. It was by contracting free labor and using black slaves of African origin, who were effective due to their physical condition and because they were used to high temperatures, that this problem could be solved.

At first, silver refining was long and costly, being based on the crushing of stones to obtain the ore, which was then smelted. In the late 16th century a miner of New Spain invented a more effective technique: amalgamation, a simpler, cheaper system which used mercury (brought from Peru and Germany) to help refine the metal.

To satisfy manufacturing needs, the Spanish first used Indians, but as their numbers dwindled and the number of whites rose, European-style guilds began to emerge to meet the demand.

Ever since the beginning of the Spanish presence, *obrajes* had been common, textile mills making cotton, silk and wool cloth, the demand for which was so great that at some periods not all the population had clothes to wear. Usually, the textiles produced in New Spain were of good quality and reasonably priced, and so most people had access to them.

There was always a rich but irregular trade between New Spain and the mother country. Commercial traffic, controlled by the Casa de Contratación in Seville, was based on the economic needs of both Spain and the viceroyalty. European products such as wine and olive oil, and Asian ones such as porcelain and jewels were exchanged for hides, silver, vanilla and cacao.

The settings for this business were the two most important ports: Acapulco and Veracruz, which received ships from both the Philippines and those which had sailed from Seville. When the foreign products reached one of these ports they were transported to Mexico City and from there redistributed to the rest of New Spain. This brought about the emergence of a solid group of merchants grouped in the Consulado, which among many other things controlled overseas trade in accordance with its needs.

During the 16th and 17th centuries the riches sent to Spain from the New World awakened the greed of pirates and privateers. To fight these, the order was given in 1529 for the treasure galleons to travel under the protection of warships.

Another of the challenges the Spanish had to face in Mesoamerica was the evangelization of its peoples. The Europeans believed that the discovery and conquest of America were rewards God had given them and that in return he demanded them to teach the natives of these lands Christian doctrine. Those responsible for carrying out this huge task were the missionaries, in other words, the regular clergy.

Between 1524 and 1576, the Franciscans, Dominicans, Augustinians and Jesuits (in this order) arrived in New Spain. The first three had a missionary tradition in Europe which, added to the poverty in which members lived, enabled them to get close to Indian communities in times when the natives were suffering so many abuses at the hands of the whites, who distrusted the orders, despite the kind of work they were doing. However, acceptance of the missionaries was also due to the fact that the Indians understood that they had little or nothing to do with the abusive encomenderos or aggressive soldiers.

The Franciscans occupied the territories of Jalisco, Mexico, Michoacán, Zacatecas, Yucatán and part of northern Veracruz; the Dominicans did their work in Chiapas, Guatemala, Mexico, Oaxaca and Puebla, while the Augustinians settled in Mexico and Michoacán. The Jesuits established schools in Mexico City and did notable missionary work among the Chichimecs in the north of the country.

The means used by the evangelists in their work were very varied, although the departure point of almost all of them was the knowledge of Indian languages. There were some who devoted themselves to evangelizing and educating the children of noble Indians, leaving the others aside. Others studied Mesoamerican beliefs, customs and rites to find parallelisms that would make teaching and learning the new religion easier. Those more versed in teaching methods did not hesitate to use songs, paintings and plays to make the Indians understand Christ's teachings. In addition, the friars left them valuable information for learning about their past through their books.

Throughout the 300 years that the viceroyalty lasted, the Church as an institution also grew thanks to the work of the secular clergy. From the start, it was organized into dioceses and ecclesiastical provinces which enabled it not only to further the process of evangelization but also to control the converts, With the passage of time, and thanks to tithes, donations, perquisites and legacies, the Catholic Church began to take possession of a good many lands and consumer goods which were managed by the secular clergy. This in turn had the reputation among members of the regular clergy of living in ostentatious luxury. It is not surprising that there were constant disputes between these two factions of the Church were during this period. What is certain is that the Church became such a strong economic power that it is estimated to have possessed one sixth of all the land in the country.

Much has been written about the Inquisition, and most of it is due to the Leyenda Negra (Black Legend) the English began telling about it in the 17th century. Established in New Spain in 1571, the Inquisition —or Court of the Holy Office— was the agency responsible for preserving Christianity in the land. People tried for the first time and found guilty were known as *lapsos* (erring) and were allowed to go free, but in the event of repeating the offense they became *relapsos* (backsliders) and were not pardoned, although the sentence was imposed by the civil authorities and not the Inquisition, and Indians could not be tried. Another part of the dark side concerns the public executions carried out by the Holy Office. It has long been believed that executions of those found guilty took place on Santo Domingo Square in Mexico City were common, but research in archives was sufficient to show that between 1571 and 1821 only 51 people were publicly executed, equivalent to about one every five years.

At the very top of New Spain's society were the Spaniards who, because of having carried out the Conquest or being descendents of them, had taken possession of the these lands. In time, two types of Spaniards were differentiated: those from Europe *(peninsulares)* and those born in Mexico *(criollos)*. The strange thing was that although the law laid down that both were Spaniards, in practice the peninsulares discriminated against the criollos.

Many of the European-born Spaniards who arrived in the country during the colonial era came with the viceroys: poor professionals wanting to make headway, opportunists who were looking to make quick fortunes and soldiers. Most of them shared the ambition to become rich, some by legal means, others illicitly. Obviously, the peninsulares held the best administrative and religious posts, and were held in high esteem by criollos, who dreamed of their daughters marrying into their families to gain prestige and improve their social status. Most peninsular Spaniards lived in the large cities of New Spain.

The criollos felt proud of being Spanish, even though the Crown allowed them to occupy only minor administrative and religious posts. This situation, irksome to the criollos, came to be so ridiculous that even a "scientific" justification was sought which held that those born in New Spain were inferior because the prevailing climate made them weak of character and there was no solution to this degenerative process.

Criollos wanted the Crown to allow them to rise to pending posts and very few thought about independence since most of them just wanted to see a change within the viceroyalty. Criollo reaction centered rather on a strong current of pride in having been born in America, which has been named *criollismo*.

For many, the great frustration of New Spain's criollos lay in the fact that they were just as Spanish as the peninsulares, had greater economic power than the Europeans, but were not admitted into political power. In short, they shared culture, traditions and a sense of belonging with the peninsulares, but were treated as second-class Spaniards.

A direct consequence of the Conquest was the emergence of mestizos, born of Spanish fathers and Indian mothers (cases of Indian fathers and Spanish mothers were rare). Since they set foot on these lands the conquistadors had had relations, voluntary or forcible, with native women, and the result of this was the birth of a large number of illegitimate children who were neither Spanish nor Indian. During the 16th and 17th centuries, the mestizos had not developed a group identity, and therefore it was common for them to mix with either Indian or Spanish society, depending on the color of their skin, with the knowledge that neither would fully accept them. This situation led to the marginalization of mestizos since in cities they could do only the lowest jobs or become robbers and beggars; in the countryside they could only cultivate land. It was not until the 18th century that the members of this group began to develop an awareness of themselves and to feel a certain degree of pride in their origins, although this did not alter their political and economic position.

One thing that underlines the peninsular Spaniards' obsession with racial purity is the system of castes. Anyone whose parents were not Spanish or Indian belonged to the world of castes. The children of a Spaniard and a mestizo woman were *castizo*; those of a Negress and a Spaniard, *mulatos*; of a mulatto woman and a Spaniard, *moriscos*; of *morisco* woman and a Spaniard, *albino*, and so on. The members of these groups were looked down on by the Spanish because of their mixed blood and therefore engaged in heavy work, domestic service or begging in the cities. At best, their only option for a decent life was field work.

The Indians led an ambivalent life because on the one hand there were numerous laws which protected them, even to the extent of considering them minors, but on the other, they were victims of the most infamous exploitation by encomenderos, owners of repartimientos and low-level public authorities. In cities, they sold their products and worked as household staff.

Finally, there were the African Negroes, who had been taken prisoner by the English and Portuguese and sold into slavery in America. Although the Indians formed a considerable workforce in New Spain, there were certain activities they could not undertake, either because of their constitution, strength or family origin. In the mines, where the temperatures at the bottom of the shaft were unbearable and where several Indians would die this every month, Africans were used because of their stamina. On haciendas and in sugar mills they were employed as overseers of Indians, which shows that relations between the two groups were not good. They also worked as servants in the houses of the wealthiest because since they were so expensive, Africans became status symbols.

The Viceroyalty (1700-1808)

The beginning of the 18th century saw a series of important changes in Spain as the result of a change of dynasty. In 1700, Charles II, the last of the Spanish Hapsburgs, died without an heir, which prompted Louis XIV of France and Joseph I of Austria to try and put a family member on the throne of Spain. As diplomatic means proved to be of little help, a struggle known as the War of the Spanish Succession broke out which was to end with the French king's victory over his Austrian enemy. Louis XIV never had the intention of leaving his country to rule Spain; on the contrary, after having triumphed he sent his grandson, Philip of Anjou, to sit on the Spanish throne. On May 8, 1701 he was crowned King of Spain under the name of Philip V and thus established the Bourbon dynasty in the country —which occupies the throne to this day.

The Bourbon kings, perhaps because of their French origins and their contact with the Enlightenment, wanted to carry out changes in Spain to turn it into a modern nation that would be able to sustain its growth with commerce and industry. The American territories played an important role in this project as they were seen as great sources of raw materials and at the same time excellent captive markets for Spain's manufactured goods. To carry out the Bourbon Reforms (the name given to the plan by the Spanish kings) they laid down the exploitation of all the productive capacity of America and the limitation of the autonomy it was showing as necessary conditions. In other words, they removed *criollos* (American-born Spaniards) from any relatively important posts they had "infiltrated."

Although customs and people's mentality evolve slowly, these reforms in New Spain brought about changes that later had serious consequences.

Fully aware of the corruption rife among the officials of New Spain, the Bourbons appointed *revisores* (auditors) and *visitadores* (royal inspectors), whose job was to audit all the agencies which managed the economic resources of the viceroyalty. As all this was not enough to increase revenue, the Spanish Crown raised taxes step by step and created new royal monopolies.

The ministers of Charles III (1759-1788) and Charles IV (1788-1808) made them see that one way to obtain more money was to step up trade between Spain and its American dominions. New ports were opened (Tampico, Mazatlán...) to encourage the entry of goods subject to tax. The policy took time to work, but when it did it brought Madrid great dividends.

The Bourbon Reforms also extended to the field of mining. Spanish intellectuals considered that mines could increase their output if those in charge of planning this activity and putting it into practice were encouraged to study. The Royal School of Mining (headquartered in what is now the Palacio de Minería in Mexico City) was founded in 1792, and through it went the first mining engineers of New Spain, who received scientific and technological training. Another important change which benefited this branch of the economy was a drop in the price of mercury, because as the price of this metal rose, silver production fell as it became unprofitable.

The Bourbons distrusted the political institutions created in America by the Hapsburgs, believing them to be too autonomous. Although their idea was not to replace all of them, they did want to make them more dependent on Spain through the intervention of a group of officials loyal to the Crown. This attitude had its repercussions in New Spain with the introduction of the system of *intendencias* (superintendencies), which marked a radical change in the viceroyalty, since the heads of these (intendants) had been educated in schools for public officials (they were no longer noble friends of the king as they had been traditionally) and in their areas enjoyed the same powers as the viceroy, a position which began to lose power and autonomy. The Audiencia was also affected since part of its judicial power passed into the hands of the intendants and in addition the *criollos*, who for some time had begun to occupy the positions of *oidores* (judges) were expelled from the Audiencia because of the Crown's suspicion of them.

If the Bourbons aimed to centralize power in Spain and America with these reforms, it is also true that they had to confront an enemy which, in their opinion, endangered the power of the Crown: the Society of Jesus. This religious order had great political and economic power in America, so much so that not a few claimed that the general of the society —its highest authority— was richer and more powerful than the king of Spain himself. In New Spain the Jesuits had influence in society because they were responsible for teaching the criollo elite in their schools, so it is not surprising that when Charles III decreed that the Society of Jesus was to be expelled from Spain and America, criollos, mestizos, Indians and the castes rose against the instruction. Their demonstrations of support served little purpose and the Jesuits finally took refuge in Italy.

To do justice to the Bourbon Reforms, the cultural streak that characterized them in New Spain must be pointed out because it was thanks to this that the ideas of the French Age of Enlightenment arrived. Since the purpose of this book is not to go into great detail about this cultural process, it is enough to say the men of the Enlightenment extolled reason above everything else as they saw in it the solution to all the ills of humankind.

The criollos educated in Jesuit schools or establishments such as the Royal and Pontifical University of Mexico, the University of Guadalajara, San Carlos College, the School of Mining, etc were those who showed most enthusiasm for the ideas of the Enlightenment. Together with the Crown of Spain they worked to spread education to the lowest classes and for this began to found lay schools and academies as well as public libraries. Science acquired importance as a means that developed reason and encouraged industry, as a fundamental element in human progress. To cite some examples, the School of Mining had the most modern instruments and books for mathematics, chemistry, physics, mineralogy and metallurgy. The Royal Academy of Surgery was founded in 1770 to train more "scientific" doctors; the teachers who worked there backed up their courses with practical anatomy lessons and in 1772 began publishing *El Mercurio Volante*, the first medical journal in all America.

This is how the final years of Mexico's life as a viceroyalty passed until the early years of the 19th century.

Chapter 3

The Struggle for Independence (1808-1821)

The Background

A war of Independence is not something organized overnight, or which occurs without any reason. Although it broke out in 1810, its background goes back some time.

As internal causes of the struggle for Independence can be cited, in the first place, the decline Spain was experiencing. Historically speaking, this nation had been typified by such a warlike spirit that it was constantly involved in wars in Europe which it financed with resources sent from America. When the House of Bourbon became established in Spain, and because it was of French origin, the Crown acquired the commitment to defend its French counterpart militarily when it was attacked by an enemy nation. The passage of years demonstrated that this "Family Pact" was more advantageous to the French, since the occasions on which Spain defended France were more numerous. These wars were very costly and the Spanish Crown was able to finance them only through a policy of forcible loans and increased taxes. In New Spain, this policy was merciless and although it affected all, the criollos were those most hurt because they formed the most economically powerful group.

Another of the Crown's clumsy or insensitive acts was the notorious Certificate of Consolidation of Royal Promissory Notes. In the viceroyal period there were no banks in New Spain; if somebody wanted a loan, he turned to the Church, which granted the request in exchange for a signed note. It is calculated that in 1804, when the certificate came into force, ninety per cent of rural properties were in debt to the Church. However, what the Crown did with the Certificate of Consolidation of Royal Promissory Notes was to take these debts away from the Church and try to call them in under the threat of confiscating properties from anyone who did not pay. Many alarmed debtors hurried to sell off other possessions cheaply to pay off their debt without knowing that the total of the note that the Spanish government held amounted to several million pesos more than the total currency in circulation in New Spain. In other words, there was not enough money in the country to pay the debts in full.

Another fact to be taken into consideration was the criollos' discontent because of the discrimination against them. American Spaniards, proud of having been born in such a rich continent, had to bear heavy taxes and were excluded from high posts in politics, the Church and the military. Their most important demand was to be given the chance to occupy eminent government posts.

Napoleon's invasion of Spain has traditionally been considered to be an external cause of the war of Independence. At the beginning of the 19th century, Bonaparte, the French emperor, wanted to impose a maritime blockade against the English, his bitter rivals. This meant that France would control all the European countries with coasts in the north because it was from there that ships would sail to prevent other vessels from entering or leaving England. By this, he would ensure that the English could not trade with their colonies and so would plunge the country into deep economic crisis which would make conquest easy. The only two nations France still needed for carrying out this plan were Spain and Portugal.

Meanwhile, things were not going well in Spain. Ever since he ascended the throne, Charles IV had shown a lack of interest and a marked incapability to rule and so always left political control in the hands of favorites or protégés. The last of these was Manuel de Godoy, a young politician who thanks to corruption and an affair with the queen. María Luisa, managed to amass a considerable fortune, occupy the post of first secretary and thus hold political control of Spain.

The king's ineptness and his secretary's ambition were factors that Napoleon turned to his advantage. In 1807 he asked the king for permission to cross Spain in order to conquer Portugal. Godoy —who the French emperor had promised a part of this last country to— persuaded Charles IV to grant permission and lend Napoleon soldiers. When Portugal was subjugated in 1808, the Spanish realized that the French, instead of leaving their territory increased their numbers in what for many was one of Napoleon's easiest victories. The public blamed Charles IV who, desperate because of his impotence to halt the invasion, abdicated in favor of his son Ferdinand, who showed greater interest in power but incompetence equal to his father's.

This was no obstacle for Napoleon, since with the aid of deception he managed to take Charles IV and Ferdinand VII to France and imprison them. Once all the Spanish royal family had been deprived of liberty, the French emperor made the son abdicate in favor of his father, and he in turn abdicate in favor of Bonaparte, who then appointed his brother Joseph king of Spain. When news of the monarchs' arrest reached Spain, at the same time as its new king was taking oath, the people took to the streets to protest. A wave of violence against the French grew in the most important Spanish cities and with it one of the cruelest repressions in history. It was May 2, 1808.

The Spanish politicians who refused to recognize Joseph I declared that while Ferdinand VII was in prison, the throne of Spain was vacant and that for this reason each province should create *juntas* which would govern in the name of the imprisoned king. The suggestion was a success and each province established its junta, which caused chaos because each body acted in its own interests and not those of the nation. To avoid this problem it was decided to create a Central Junta in Cadiz to be the head of its local counterparts and issue orders about what they should do.

When news of the imprisonment and abdication of Ferdinand VII reached New Spain, fear took hold of the political class and the criollos. What should they do so as not to betray the king? Factions emerged rapidly. The criollos defended the position that a *junta* should be organized in the name of Ferdinand VII, although they did not say that they were to control it. On their part, the peninsular Spaniards decided that the royal *Acuerdo* (an assembly composed of the viceroy, the Audiencia and the archbishop of Mexico City) was to govern until such time as the picture in Spain became clear.

The situation became tense when the viceroy, José de Iturrigaray refused to support any of the parties. The peninsulares took this to be a sign of his support for the criollos who, according to the Europeans, wanted to take advantage of the situation to proclaim the viceroyalty's independence. It was because of this that on the night of September 15, 1808, a group of Spanish merchants forced their way into the governor's palace, took the viceroy prisoner together with his family.

From this time on the criollos began to brand the government of Mexico City as illegitimate because it represented neither the king nor the people of New Spain. It must also be pointed out that this rejection was the result of the frustration of the Spanish Americans who saw their dreams of attaining power evaporate. Refusing to sit with their arms crossed, the criollos most dedicated to the move to establish a junta in the viceroyalty began to organize conspiracies in different parts of the country as from 1809. These plots (in Celaya, San Miguel el Grande, Valladolid and elsewhere) all shared certain elements: they agreed that the Mexico City government had to be eliminated if they were to achieve their aims; there was also a criollo majority ready to be sacrificed but the plots were found out before they could erupt.

Hidalgo's Movement (1810-1811)

The most famous of all these groups was the Querétaro one (1810), regarded as the beginning of the movement for Mexico's independence. Ignacio Allende, Juan Aldama, Miguel Domínguez, Josefa Ortíz de Domínguez —better known as La Corregidora because she was married to the *corregidor* of Querétaro— and Miguel Hidalgo were the most famous members. The parish priest Hidalgo was the last to join the

Miguel Hidalgo.

confabulation and this was due to the intervention of his friend Igna-cio Allende who, aware that a priest's involvement would help draw more people into the movement, invited him to join.

Miguel Hidalgo y Costilla was an unorthodox priest. Born of a good family and living in the small town of Dolores this enlightened criollo was concerned about the needs of his poorest parishioners and about helping them by setting up potteries, encouraging them to grow mulberry trees to feed silkworms, teaching music and acting, etc.

The conspirators planned to begin the uprising in December 1810, but in September that year the Spanish authorities were alerted to the existence of the Querétaro plot and acted to put an end to it. When the first criollos were detained the conspirators began to wonder whether they should take up arms or give themselves up to the authorities. Hidalgo was charged with making the decision. In the early hours of Sunday, September 16, 1810, together with Abasolo and Allende, he rang the bells of his church and urged his parishioners to take up arms with them. This event is known as *El grito* (The Cry) and is still celebrated year after year on September 15. Tradition has it that by this

51

act Hidalgo called upon all Mexicans to rise and fight against the bad government of Spain, against the *gachupines* (as the common people called the peninsular Spaniards) and in favor of independence. However, he could not have appealed to "Mexicans" because Mexico did not exist as a country and the only "Mexicans" were the inhabitants of the capital of the viceroyalty. Bad government was referred to, but meaning that of Mexico City because it had arisen from a coup d'état; he could not have declared independence because most versions of the event agree that a fundamental part of this call was "long live Ferdinand VII". This movement obviously wanted to seize power in order to create a criollo governing council.

From the start the clear aims of Hidalgo's uprising were first to take the city of Guanajuato and then Mexico City. The mutiny was also attractive to the poor majorities of the central region of New Spain because they were made happy and confident by the fact that a priest was its leader, that the banner of the Virgin of Guadalupe was its emblem and that they were being given the chance to fight the Spaniards.

Criollos in the rest of the viceroyalty looked on the movement with approval at first because they understood that they were going to be allowed to have access to political power. This feeling changed when news of what had happened in the Alhóndiga de Granaditas at the end of September spread through New Spain. Located in Guanajuato, a vital point in the viceroyalty, this public granary was used by the Spaniards as shelter from the imminent arrival of Hidalgo and his makeshift army of 50,000 men. After a bloody siege, the armed rebels managed to defeat the resistance and entered the area to kill the survivors; not content with this the disorderly mob took to the streets of Guanajuato to loot houses and stores. This chaos could only be brought under control when Allende forcibly imposed order. These events, unheard of in New Spain, made the criollos withdraw their support from Hidalgo, because they were interested in gaining political control they did not want it at the cost of violence and disorder. In addition, others thought that what had occurred in Guanajuato could well happen in Mexico City, the proud capital of the viceroyalty, causing ominous consequences for New Spain.

This did not matter to Hidalgo since as his army marched toward Mexico City it grew until it contained the staggering figure of 80,000 men. It was only to be expected that the viceroyal army would fail in all is attempts to halt such a contingent. On October 30, the Spanish and rebel troops clashed on the Cerrro de las Cruces (today in Cuajimalpa) in what was Hidalgo's last obstacle before Mexico City. After a battle lasting six hours the Spanish troops were defeated and everything was ready for the occupation of the city. It was at this moment that history gave an unexpected twist. On October 31, Hidalgo made a decision which surprised everybody: he ordered a retreat. Why did he retreat when the ultimate aim was about to be achieved? Hidalgo never explained.

In November 1810, as a result of the above move, Hidalgo and Allende decided to separate. The former marched to the city of Guadalajara and the latter to Guanajuato. The separation did not benefit either of then since Allende was defeated time after time by the royalist army and Hidalgo devoted himself to legal matters, completely forgetting the military issue, so important for the existence of the uprising. In January 1811 the two leaders met again to strengthen the movement and present a united front against the royalist general Félix María Calleja, who was very close to Guadalajara. The confrontation took place on January, 1811 at Puente de Calderón and the Spanish troops were victorious. Calleja not only defeated Hidalgo and Allende, but literally finished off their army by capturing most of its officers and taking possession of almost all its cannons. Hidalgo and Allende escaped almost by a miracle and after meeting up again in the present day state of Aguascalientes decided to go north and ask the United States for military and economic assistance. The project could never be carried out because they were taken prisoner in Acatitla del Baján (today, Baján, Coahuila), tried —Hidalgo, being a priest, was tried by an ecclesiastical court— and condemned to death. Allende, Aldama and another rebel called Mariano Jiménez faced the firing squad on June 26, and one month later, Hidalgo met the same fate. The viceroy ordered the heads

José María Morelos.

of the four placed in cages and hung at the four corners of the Alhóndiga de Granaditas as an example to everybody of what could happen
to those who rose against him.

The Movement of Morelos (1811 - 1815)

Once Hidalgo was dead, another priest took charge of the movement.
José María Morelos y Pavón was a mestizo of humble origin who took
up the priesthood when he was aged over 30 and who, like Hidalgo,
was very aware of the injustices and backwardness suffered by the
people. What is interesting about Morelos is that unlike his fellow priest,
since 1814 he wanted to create a new homeland where Americans,
regardless of their origin would be the ones to govern. The irony is
that Hidalgo is called "the father of the homeland," a title which should
rightfully be given to Morelos.

Morelos was a great military strategist, a fact which has been used
by historians to group his fighting activities into campaigns. The first

54

was from 1810 to 1811, the second from 1811 to 1812, the third from 1812 to 1813 and the last from 1813 to 1815. The first three marked Morelos's successful stage, while the fourth was that of defeat.

In his initial campaign, Morelos acted in the south of the country, in what is now the state of Guerrero. This was when the leader of the insurgent —as those who had been under arms since 1811 were known— organized a small, well-run army (to avoid the disorderliness typical of Hidalgo's troops) led by such trusted officers as the Bravo and Galeana brothers.

The second campaign was characterized by the political and military hegemony Morelos's army maintained in the central and southern parts of New Spain. The siege of Cuautla dates from this period In February 1812, general Calleja made the decision to lay siege to the town of Cuautla because Morelos and his men were there. The idea of the royalist —as those who fought the insurgents were called— was to force the rebel leader to surrender once his food ran out. However, Morelos did not surrender and after seventy days broke through the cordon when the Spanish was least expecting it and managed to escape with most of his men. As this story spread through the viceroyalty, Morelos's popularity grew until it reached mythic proportions.

The third campaign was important for several reasons. In theory, a large part of southeast New Spain was under the control of the insurgents, while Calleja was appointed viceroy to capture Morelos and put an end to his movement once and for all. But it was also the time when he wrote *Sentimientos de la Nación* (1813), a short text expressing his political thoughts. He stated that América del Septentrión —as he called New Spain— was independent of Spain, that those who were natives of these lands would have the same rights and that only they would be able to aspire to political posts. To give this document more force he created a Congress in the town of Chilpancingo which proclaimed the independence of New Spain. Independence was mentioned for the first time.

The last stage was one of contrasts, because while the rebels made political progress such as the *Constitution of Apatzingán*, the first document to give the "new nation" a system of government with a division of power and popular rule, they suffered defeat after defeat in the military sphere. Several factors helped toward this situation. Calleja began the systematic pursuit of Morelos, his followers and the Congress, while these two leaders had problems of military command, problems which ended when the organization took authority away from the "serf of the Nation" as Morelos was also known. There is no doubt that luck was also an important factor, for if between 1811 and 1813 it had favored the insurgents, from 1814 on it was against them. In 1815, when the Congress was fleeing from Calleja its members, Morelos included, were captured and after trial, condemned to death. Morelos was executed by a firing squad at San Cristóbal Ecatepec near Mexico City on December 22, 1814.

The Leaderless Interlude (1815 - 1820)

After the death of Morelos there was no insurgent strong enough to become the head of the movement. Men such as Guadalupe Victoria, Vicente Guerrero, Ignacio López Rayón, Pedro Moreno, Father Torres were leaders whose power was only local and, because of quarrels among themselves, did not wish to assume such a heavy commitment. As was to be expected, this situation benefited the royalists, who reoccupied the territory lost and left the different rebel leaders cut off on small "islands."

The situation was affected momentarily in 1817 when a young Spaniard landed in New Spain determined to bring it independence. He was Martín Javier Mina, a Spanish liberal who fought against the French in the Napoleonic invasion with such tenacity that by the time he was 19 he was regarded as a hero. In 1810 he was taken prisoner and set free four years later, only days before Ferdinand VII returned to govern his country and the French began to leave Spain. Being the liberal he was, he agreed that the Central Assembly of Cadiz should proclaim a Constitution in 1812 limiting the powers of the kings of Spain and giving the people sovereignty. When Ferdinand VII returned to his country he swore allegiance to the Constitution but abolished it after two months in his own interest and began a campaign against the liberals because they had encouraged it.

Despite his background of patriotism, Mina was persecuted and was able to avoid imprisonment only by leaving Spain in 1815. He took refuge in England and made contact with some dissident exiles from New Spain who persuaded him to go and fight for the country's independence.

The expedition sailed from England in late 1816 and reached New Spain in 1817. Actually, Mina could do little since it took several days to find rebel groups that wanted to help; he had few arms and soldiers and was being pursued by the royalists. His intentions were simple: to go to the city of Guanajuato and from there march on Mexico City, take it and proclaim independence. However, nothing of this could be done because when he was nearing Guanajuato he was taken prisoner. The viceroy, at that time Juan Ruiz de Apodaca was well aware of Mina's fame as a patriot and before he could attract royalist troops to his cause, gave orders for him to be shot without trial on November 11, 1817, on the Cerro del Sombrerete.

The importance of this man, who was really able to do little, lies in the example he gave. When news of his arrival was made public, many natives of New Spain who had deserted the rebel cause through fear or apathy felt affected. How could a Spaniard come to fight for their cause? Mina revived the independence movement, however modestly, and this was the incursion's success.

The two years following Mina's death passed without any great change. True, more insurgent groups arose but they were purely local and none of them was able to become a wide, unifying movement. This began to change once again however in 1820 as a result of events in Spain.

Iturbide's Movement and the Consummation of Independence (1820 - 1821)

On January 1, 1820, Colonel Rafael de Riego and the troops under his command rose against King Ferdinand VII in Spain. Since 1815, groups of military men, merchants, nobles, intellectuals and priests, all of them liberals, had been plotting against the king for being an absolutist monarch. However, none of these plots bore fruit. Riego's position was different. He was a liberal. Was in agreement with American independence since he believed that it could not be stopped and in addition was in Cadiz, waiting to be sent to fight against insurgents in the viceroyalty of Río de la Plata, Argentina. Against this background, the colonel made the decision to organize an armed struggle of a constitutionalist nature that would put an end to absolute monarchy in Spain and incidentally save him the voyage to America. When news of Riego's revolt spread through the Iberian peninsula other liberals followed his example and took up arms in favor of restoring the 1812 Constitution. Fernando VII paid no attention to these events at first, but when the garrison of Madrid rebelled in March he gave up and the same month accepted the Constitution for the second time. This meant that the king had to share power with the triumphant party, in other words, the liberals.

When news of what had happened in Spain reached New Spain in July, a section of the elite were satisfied because they saw it meant great strides forward. The criollos thought that the new liberal government was going to make considerable changes which would be to their advantage; some peninsulares thought that things would improve politically with the end of absolute monarchy. However, none of these expectations were realized. The government of Spain behaved toward the criollos just as it had in the times of absolutism, continuing to ignore their political demands; things did not go well for the peninsulares either because the new authorities suppressed military prerogatives —the right of army members to be tried by their own courts— and eliminated the proofs of *hidalguería* (nobility) for all those who wished to occupy public offices. Neither did the clergy escape unharmed since the Jesuits were expelled for the second time and a policy was planned to secularize Church property both in Spain and America.

Criollos and peninsular Spaniards, laymen and clerics, ordinary citizens and officials saw how the Constitution affected their interests, without having the means to defend themselves. This was when they reached an agreement: it was time to unite in a struggle for independence. They met in La Profesa church, Mexico City, and agreed that to bring their plans to fruition they had to unify the insurgent movement, a delicate task which had to be entrusted to someone capable and intelligent. Those present agreed that there was only one person who had these qualities: Agustín de Iturbide. He was a criollo who from the beginning of the conflict had fought very successfully for the Spanish Crown. The rebels knew him very well since he was notorious for having no mercy toward them. When he was offered the chance to unify the insurgent movement and bring about independence he accepted immediately.

Iturbide realized that his first step had to be to get close to an important rebel who was well-known among those who had fought for independence. He chose Vicente Guerrero, a mulatto who since the time of Morelos had fought in the state which now bears his surname. Iturbide went to the territory of the rebel leader to talk to him and draw him into his cause. He convinced Guerrero that the only way to bring independence about was to cement a union between them. This was made official when the two leaders and their troops met in the village of Acatempan. There, Guerrero and Iturbide embraced each other and signed the *Plan de Iguala*, a document that established the basic principles for governing the future Empire of Mexico. An important point of this was that the crown would be offered to the king of Spain or, if he were unable to accept it, to one of his family members.

This might seem to be a contradiction, but Iturbide did not see it so since what he wanted was a separation from Spain that would give the criollos power without there being a complete break from the Spanish heritage.

As from this moment, Iturbide carried out a dual campaign. By day he used arms against those who opposed him and at night wrote letters to important military, religious and political figures urging them to join his cause. In late 1820 and early 1821 it was obvious that the second policy had been the most effective: bishops and important military leaders such as Antonio López de Santa Anna, Anastasio Bustamante and Manuel Gómez Pedraza, all fervent royalists had gone over to his side. Iturbide, in a daring stroke, invited the viceroy to join him, but he declined the offer, being a staunch supporter of the Crown.

When Iturbide controlled all the viceroyalty except Mexico City and Veracruz, the new viceroy landed in New Spain. He was Juan O'Donjú, a liberal who sympathized with the cause for independence and who, as a soldier, knew that everything was lost for Spain. This explains why when Iturbide asked him for an audience the request was granted.

In August 1821 the two met in the town of Córdoba, Veracruz, and O'Donjú agreed to sign the Treaties named for the location. These documents ratified the *Plan de Iguala* except for one point: it was specified that if the king of Spain did not come or send a family member to sit on the throne of Mexico, Mexicans would choose their emperor.

After the *Treaty of Córdoba* had been signed, the insurgents made for Mexico City. Because of the strength and size of the rebel army, the royalist troops defending the capital put up no resistance. At 11 a.m. on September 27, 1821, the insurgents entered Mexico City and thus affirmed the country's independence.

During the life of the Viceroyalty of New Spain, the mother country sent 62 viceroys to Mexico City. These included good rulers, others who were frankly bad or mediocre, and some who simply looked after their own interests.

Chapter 4

From the First Empire to the War with the United States (1821 - 1848)

The First Empire (1821 - 1823)

The arrival of the insurgents in Mexico City was a cause for celebration because for many people it meant the end of a long struggle. Despite this, there was a minority who were worried because they thought it simply marked the beginning of a more delicate and equally important process: the building of a nation.

The first measure taken was to form a provisional junta responsible for governing the country until there was an emperor. Immediately afterward, a letter was sent to Ferdinand VII inviting him or a member of his family to accept the throne of the Mexican Empire.

It was only a matter of days before ideological differences began to show themselves and evidence of this was the Congress, created to affirm legislative power. Three currents could be seen in it: monarchists, republicans and Bourbonists. The first supported the moderate monarchy proposed in the *Plan de Iguala* and the *Treaty of Córdoba* and were not against the idea of Iturbide finally crowning himself emperor. The republicans, for the most part insurgents who had fought for the cause since 1811 and 1812 were afraid that the empire would end by becoming an absolutist rule controlled by Iturbide; their proposal was to copy the government pattern of the United States, a model they thought

The first emperor
of Mexico,
Agustín de Iturbide.

worth emulating. The Bourbonists were in the middle, being ready to support either of these options, depending on who the monarch was. They made it clear that if a king of the house of Bourbon did not come to rule, they preferred a republican government.

The situation grew worse when the king of Spain's answer arrived: neither he nor any of his family would sit on the throne of Mexico insofar as they did not recognize New Spain's independence. Although some people had been predicting this answer for some time, the news fell on Mexico like a bucket of cold water because it altered all the plans. On the other hand, Iturbide's supporters were overjoyed at the news because they saw their leader as becoming the highest authority in the country. Things came to a head on the evening of May 18, 1822. A group of soldiers went out into the streets of Mexico City —incited by Iturbide himself some people said—. Shouting "Long live Agustín I, emperor of Mexico!" The populace supported the proclamation and in the morning so did the army. Faced with such pressure, Congress declared Iturbide emperor without even having finished drawing up the Constitution that was to govern the empire.

From then on, relations between Iturbide and Congress grew strained. To begin with, members of the legislative power were annoyed because such pressure had been exerted for the coronation, but this situation also altered their duties: now they had to discuss titles of nobility, the emperor's court, etc., and leave the Constitution to one side. The issue causing the most tension between the two powers was the question of budget because after having calculated that total tax revenue for 1822 would be 11 million pesos, not enough for the government to work at its best, the emperor wanted 10 million to be earmarked for the army, his loyal support. As there was no Magna Carta specifying the rights of each power, the controversy could not be surmounted until Iturbide arbitrarily gave himself the power to veto the decisions of the Congress.

These disputes cost the emperor followers in the Congress and in consequence, republican ideas began to gain strength in plots to overthrow the emperor. More than a year after independence Iturbide could not rule his empire because he had to uncover plots and imprison subversive congressmen. The only way he found to manage the issue of government was to dissolve the legislative branch (Congress) and replace it by a Council of Notables made up of the few friends he had left.

The political situation was so hot that the army decided it should intervene to put an end to it. As Iturbide was no longer of any use to them, in December 1822 they organized an armed uprising led by Antonio López de Santa Anna. The protesters signed the *Plan de Veracruz* repudiating Iturbide and proposing a republican form of government. The movement was joined by famous old insurgents such as Vicente Guerrero, Guadalupe Victoria and Nicolás Bravo. At the beginning of 1823 the emperor, who had given no importance to the movement before, yielded to the pressure of events, abdicated and with his family sought refuge in Italy. Later he returned to Mexico in an attempt to recover power but was apprehended then finally shot in Padilla, Tamaulipas.

The First Federal Republic (1824 - 1835)

The emperor's departure signified a triumph for the republican movement. The victors decided to create a provisional government until such time as the Congress reassembled and gave the country a Constitution. This Supreme Executive Power was known as the triumvirate because it had three members: Nicolás Bravo, Guadalupe Victoria and Pedro Celestino Negrete —the last was the only president of the country born in Spain.

Within the Congress, arguments centered around the question of what type of republic Mexico was going to be. The old monarchists argued for a centralized republic, in other words the creation of a government which would take autonomy away from the states and order them what to do; the original republicans proposed federalism, a form of government under which the states would have the possibility of making certain decisions without the need to consult the central authority or obtain its consent. The two systems had their advantages and disadvantages. During the viceroyalty Mexico had been governed on centralist lines, so this way of ruling the country was not new and fitted in with the nation's past, but obviously the disadvantage was the anger it would cause in the different states at their lack of autonomy. Federalism had the virtue of giving local authorities more independence in a country which covered over four million square kilometers (more than double Mexico's area nowadays). The problem lay in the fact that this type of republic could weaken the union of the country. The debate on this subject was overcome, not because the congressmen of one side won over those of the other but because of the pressure exerted by the states of Oaxaca, Jalisco, Yucatán and Zacatecas, which threatened to secede from Mexico if centralism were adopted. This was enough to make the Congress decide that Mexico would be a federal republic.

Once the form of government was decided, the legislative power proceeded to give the nation its first Constitution, promulgated on October 4, 1824. In contrast to the current Magna Carta, the *Constitution of 1824* laid great weight on the political and administrative organization of the nation, while the question of recognizing and respecting the rights of Mexicans was relegated to second place —which shows the real concerns of Mexican politicians at the time.

Then the Congress called elections for Mexico's first president. It should be noted that at the time, elections were not universal as they are today; the only ones to vote were members of the Congress. The winner was Guadalupe Victoria, whose real name was José Ramón Fernández y Félix.

Since the time of the Independence, Victoria had always been known as an even-tempered man who wanted to make compromises in order to unify, as far as possible. This was evident during his term of office. Knowing that the Mexican political class was dividing he tried, at least at the beginning, to show he was going to govern for everyone, not just for the federalists; proof of this was his cabinet, which was made up of federalists and moderate centralists. Thanks to this policy, Victoria's presidency was one of the most stable in the first half of the 19th century.

This period of administration saw several outstanding achievements. In 1825 the United States and England were persuaded to recognize Mexico's independence and establish diplomatic and commercial relations. Also, the Federal District, the state of Tlaxcala, the first Board of Public Education in the country's history and the Supreme Court of Justice were created and furthermore the foundations were laid for the future creation of a national history museum.

It would be very rash to say that Victoria's term of office was perfect because it generated certain problems. This was the era of Masonic lodges, which in actual fact worked like the political parties of today. The centralists attached themselves to the Scottish Rite Lodge, which had a strong pro-Spanish leaning. This angered the federalists, including Victoria himself, who with the help of the U.S. ambassador Joel R. Poinsett, created the York Rite Lodge which, besides having a federalist tendency, adopted an anti-Spanish stance to rival the Scottish Rite Masons. Victoria ended by falling into this game of lodges and to weaken his political rivals issued the *Decree on the expulsion of Spaniards* in 1827. There was much talk that the Spaniards in Mexico were conspiring for Ferdinand VII to recover control of the land and it was even made public that a priest —Fray Juan de Arenas— was at the head of one of these plots. Although the decree was not applied fully all over the country it did cause damage because the Spaniards who were forced to leave sold all their property and took their money away with them. This began a capital flight which had a serious effect on Mexico's already weakened economy.

After four years of this administration the Congress in 1829 to choose a new president. Ten candidates stood for office, all federalists and renowned military men, but only two of them stood any great chance; Manuel Gómez Pedraza and Vicente Guerrero. Because of his education and origin (criollo) the members of Congress chose the first, but before he could take office Guerrero, with the help of Santa Anna, threatened an armed rebellion if he were not appointed president. On seeing that the army supported the rebel leader, Congress took the appointment away from Gómez Pedraza and gave it to Guerrero.

Guerrero's administration was characterized by being very troubled as a result of the president's lack of political skill and because of the hostility that certain strata of society felt toward him. In his eagerness to have a conciliatory cabinet he wished to gather federalists and centralists together in it, but opinions in it were so different that the cabinet became an obstacle to government. The upper class of the country who controlled the most important printed media could not accept that a mulatto, uneducated and politically illegitimate should rule them in convincing proof that social prejudices had not disappeared with the coming of independence.

The criticism leveled at the president made him act more impulsively and dig his own grave more rapidly. In 1829 the *Decree on the Abolition of Slavery* was issued without taking into account the fact that colonists in Texas, characterized by their rebellious spirit, had only slaves as their labor force, and such was their displeasure that they threatened independence. Guerrero had to pull back. A year later, despite knowing what the economic consequences would be, he issued the *Second Decree on the Expulsion of Spaniards* in a fruitless attempt to increase his political "points".

One praiseworthy act the in term of office of Guerrero was that in 1829 he honorably confronted the invasion by Barradas, a Spanish general who sailed from Cuba with three thousand Spanish soldiers and landed at Tampico to attempt the reconquest of New Spain. Guerrero lost no time and organized the defense of the country in what can be considered a resounding success for national troops because the invaders were forced to embark again after being defeated.

The dissatisfaction of both civilians and the military with Guerrero was so great that the triumph above was minimized, and in contrast, a centralist military uprising organized by Santa Anna who demanded his resignation for the repeated violation of the law, failure to pay the troops and the anarchy that prevailed in the country. He also demanded that General Anastasio Bustamante, until then vice-president should take his place. Guerrero id not consent to this and decided to fight his opponents in what was the first civil war Mexico had ever experienced. The conflict ended in 1831 when Guerrero was betrayed in Acapulco and executed by firing squad in Cuilapan.

Bustamante functioned as president from 1831 to 1832. Those who brought him to power stated that his job would to be to bring order to the country regardless of the means and he obediently offered to fulfill the orders in the only way he knew how, By means of harshness and bloodshed, Buatamante made it his business to pacify the nation by eliminating his federalist opponents..

Within the army there were men who were against Bustamente because they thought they were more qualified than him to govern. One of these was Antonio López de Santa Anna, who firmly believed that the president had not rewarded him sufficiently for having helped him ascend to power. Together with other renowned soldiers he organized a revolt in which he demanded the recognition of Manuel Gómez Pedraza as legitimate president of Mexico. Why did he now demand that the man he had risen against years earlier should now occupy the presidency? Santa Anna considered that the time had come for him to be president, but he wanted to hold the office as the result of an electoral triumph, not an armed one. Therefore, Gomez Pedraza became an instrument for attaining power. The revolt was seconded all over the country and this was enough to make Bustamante resign.

Gómez Pedraza was president of Mexico for three months, the time left for the presidential period to run its course which he should have headed since the beginning. In early 1833 Congress called elections and Santa Anna won a resounding victory, as was to be expected. For his vice-president he chose Valentín Gómez Farías, a fervent partisan of the Progress Party.

This was formed in the early 1830s to provide a political proposal different from that of the York Rite and Scottish Rite Masons. Inspired by the ideas of the Enlightenment, José María Luis Mora and Luis de la Rosa founded the Progress Party to transform the country radically and ensure, as the name indicated, its future progress through the application of a series of principles, namely: absolute freedom of opinion and the press, the abolition of military and ecclesiastical *fueros* (exempting clergymen and military personnel from being tried in civil courts), the suppression of monasteries, taking civil affairs such as weddings and funerals away from the clergy, the creation of more landowners to foster the circulation of wealth, to take the monopoly of education away from the Church and establish more public libraries and museums to educate the population.

The first decision Santa Anna made on being proclaimed president of Mexico was to retire to his hacienda in Veracruz *Manga de Clavo* and leave power, as the law laid down, in the hands of Gómez Farías. As a faithful follower of the Progress Party, the vice-president thought the time had come to initiate the total transformation of the country, and for this issued a series of progressive reforms in 1833 which proposed the voluntary payment of tithes, the voluntary exercise of religious vows (chastity, obedience and poverty), the closure of the Pontifical University of Mexico and the creation of the Department of Public Education. The purpose of all these provisions was clear: to weaken the Church which he blamed for all the ills and backwardness Mexico suffered from.

The reforms were too advanced for a population that was not ready for them, and did not want them either. Mexico City was the scene of a

Antonio López de
Santa Anna.

revolt of considerable size in which the clergy, the army and the populace took part. Faced with this grave situation, Gómez Farías sent a letter to Santa Anna asking him to return and reestablish order. The general returned to the capital a few days later, rescinded these reforms and to calm tempers, ordered Gómez Farías expelled from the country.

These measures did not help to restore order, since the centralists, who saw the opportunity to topple the federalist regime, began to incite the populace to rise against it as they blamed them for all the nation's problems. Faced with these successful calls, in 1835 Congress decided the time had come to make the transition to centralism. The legislative power became a constituent congress, since the centralism had to have a Constitution of the same kind.

The Centralist Republic (1835 - 1846 and the Independence of Texas

While debates were going on in Congress, a serious problem surfaced in the north of the country: the independence of Texas.

One of the greatest problems Texas had faced in viceroyal times was lack of population. So that the land could be exploited, the Spanish Crown had encouraged the establishment of foreign colonies. Although one of the conditions was that they should be Roman Catholics, most of the people who settled there were Anglo-Saxon Protestants (nowadays they would be called Americans) who, in order to receive land, swore they were Catholics. With independence, the Mexican government followed the policy of immigration, while the North American government began to finance the settlement of colonists loyal to it.

There were several problems involved since at the beginning, no Mexican authority supervised this process of colonization and consequently it was uncontrolled. Furthermore, the governments of Mexico showed no interest in Texas since it was very far from the capital, and this enabled the Texans to enjoy a degree of autonomy they soon became used to and were able to talk of seceding from Mexico.

After several warnings, the colonists took up arms against Mexico in March 1836 and set themselves up as a republic, with Sam Houston as president. Santa Anna decided to punish the rebels and for this gathered together a makeshift army in San Luis Potosí, badly equipped and without the necessary provisions which he pushed through Mexico to Texas by a series of forced marches. There he fought several battles against the enemy, the most famous being that of "El Álamo" a fort in San Antonio, since by order of Santa Anna the Mexican troops executed all the survivors they found.

When it seemed that Mexico were going to win the war, its army was caught in a surprise attack. Santa Anna was later captured and forced to sign the *Velasco Treaties* under which, without having the authority to do so, he granted Texas its independence. When he returned to Mexico City the general was repudiated and branded a traitor, a situation the centralists took advantage of to give more force to their arguments against federalism.

By this time, King Ferdinand VII was dead and Spain finally recognized Mexico's independence, and the treaty was signed in Madrid.

On December 30, 1836, Congress enacted the *Seven Laws* (also known as the *Constitution of 1836*). This document mentioned the Supreme Conservative Power, an organism created to supervise the other three political powers (executive, legislative and judicial) and limited the rights of the states of the republic.

In 1837, Congress appointed Anastasio Bustamante president because many of its members had good memories of him and continued to believe ha was the only person who could bring order to the country. But Bustamante was a different man and instead of governing with an iron hand, decided to compromise with centralists, federalists and progressives to prevent another coup d'état overthrowing him.

This change of attitude by the president was of little use since the federalists, who wished to return to power, systematically began to organize uprisings in the north and center of the country. To this must be added other disasters such as earthquakes, floods and epidemics which happened all over the country.

In 1838, when the situation was critical, Bustamante had to face an international conflict; French ships reached the port of Veracruz in 1838 and began attacking it. The reasons for this aggression went back to 1830 when the French government recognized Mexico's independence and forwarded a loan in exchange for receiving "most favored nation" treatment, which meant that France would receive trading privileges that no other country had, The Mexican government never complied with its part of the commitment and on the contrary affected the economic interests of the French. In addition to applying a policy of forced loans from French citizens living in Mexico, the constant uprisings and revolts were destroying their businesses, houses and other property.

In 1837, the French citizens complained about this to their ambassador, who demanded that the government pay substantial compensation to make up for the losses of his compatriots in the country. The Mexican government refused and by doing this provided the motive for the French to send their ships and soldiers to Veracruz in what is known as the First French Intervention.

When Santa Anna, who was on his hacienda, heard about the attack on Veracruz he decided to act without the political and military authorities asking him. He appeared in the port and tried to negotiate with the Europeans but no agreement was reached that was satisfactory to both parties. Cannon fire on Veracruz increased and the French proceeded to disembark. When Santa Anna tried to repel the invaders a cannonball seriously damaged his left leg, which had to be amputated below the knee. This marked the end of the war, since in 1839 Mexico had to begin peace talks. The government undertook to pay the damages demanded and the loan extended by France in 1830. The person who benefited most from this fight was Santa Anna, for he stopped being the traitor of the war against Texas and became the hero of the war with France, because he had been ready to sacrifice the completeness of his body for the completeness of the country.

A month after an end had been put to the French intervention, Bustamante saw Yucatán proclaim its independence from Mexico for the first time. The reasons put forward to justify this action were that with the arrival of centralism, the state had lost economic privileges it had always had because it was one of the poorest regions of the country. At first the government tried to negotiate a solution to the problem, but on being unsuccessful opted to use force, beginning an attack by land and blockading all the peninsula's ports. This measure failed, and it was only after another round of talks that Yucatan reunited with Mexico in 1843.

This could not go on for much longer. The country was sunk in a chaotic situation such as it had never seen before; internal quarrels increased, and meanwhile the country was falling to pieces without the authorities being able to prevent it. In 1841 there was a military uprising in Guadalajara against Bustamante and the Constitution of 1836. The president did not want to be a factor of discord for a second time and when he learned of this movement he went into exile.

The rebels proclaimed Santa Anna president of Mexico and in 1842 he invited Congress to provide the nation with a new Constitution. These were times characterized by the way of a political leader from Veracruz governing on the edge of the law. He wanted to suppress the independence of Congress, he absented himself from the capital several times without its permission and had governors who refused to carry au his orders imprisoned.

Such a dictatorship could not have a good ending. In 1844 another armed revolt broke out in Guadalajara which sent Santa Anna into exile and raised General José Joaquín Herrera. He was able to do little to govern because of the threat of a war against the United States, a country which did not hide its ambition to annex Mexican territory, and constant federalist uprisings.

The Second Federal Republic (1846-1848) and the War with the United States.

There was another army rebellion in 1845 which ended the following year when Congress recognized General Mariano Paredes as president. He prepared the country to face a war with the United States that he considered unavoidable. His efforts were of little use since at the time war broke out, Yucatán declared its independence for a second time and a federalist revolt toppled him and replaced him with Santa Anna once again, who in turn chose Valentín Gómez Farías as his vice-president..

Ever since the 1840s the policy of the American government had been an expansionist one and Mexico played an important role in it. In

1845 the American authorities sent envoys to Mexico City to find out whether the government was prepared to sell Upper California and New Mexico for twenty million dollars (or pesos, because at that time the two currencies were on a par). The instability prevailing in the country made it impossible for these representatives to make the government an offer and therefore they returned to their country empty-handed. The U.S. president of the time, James K. Polk, realized it would be easier to acquire these territories by war than try to buy them.

In May, 1846, a group of North American soldiers went into Mexican territory without authorization and when they came up against Mexican troops there was a skirmish in which no one was killed. Clearly, it was provocation for Mexico and it served Polk as an excuse to declare war, stating that the Mexican troops had invaded U.S. territory.

The North American army invaded Upper California while Santa Anna once more tried to scrape an army together and obtain funds to maintain it. The advance to the south of the Americans under General Zachary Taylor was overwhelming; the improvised Mexican army's lack of preparation contributed toward this. Soon after the war had started and after defeating the Mexican troops at Palo Alto and Resaca de la Palma. The Americans were in Monterrey. Santa Anna decided to make northward, leaving Gómez Farías as interim president with the instruction to obtain resources to face a war. On February 22 and 23, 1846, the Mexican army attacked the North Americans at La Angostura but on the brink of victory Santa Anna absurdly ordered a retreat.

Gómez Farías judged that the fastest, easiest and most convenient way (for the liberals) to obtain funds was to take them from the Church. Therefore, in January, 1847 he issued a law authorizing the government to appropriate Church goods until it had amassed 15 million pesos. The reaction was similar to the one seen ten years earlier. The people and clergy rose in arms and Mexico City became a battlefield where the angry crowds prevented Gómez Farías from leaving the National Palace. The situation was so bad that Santa Anna had to leave the front, where he had suffered only defeat, and go to the rescue of his vice-president. Once in the city he annulled the decree that had caused the unrest and replaced it with a "voluntary" contribution from the clergy of 100 thousand pesos.

To end the war, the North Americans opened another battle front by invading the port of Veracruz. Now the invaders were attacking the country in the north and the southeast, and the Mexican army were powerless to halt their advance.

By mid 1847 it was almost a certain fact that the invaders would enter Mexico City, so the political authorities, headed by the president made preparations to prevent this happening. All the entrances were reinforced, especially the northern ones, with troops, members of the national guard and volunteers. On September 7, the first clashes occurred at Casa Mata, Molino del Rey and Churubusco... but the most famous took place on September 13 at Chapultepec Castle, at that time the Military Academy. There, the young cadets and the American army fought in an unequal battle from which the foreign troops emerged victorious. Since the end of the 19th century the six young cadets who died heroically during the assault on Chapultepec have been know as *Los Niños Héroes* (The Boy Heroes).

The fall of Chapultepec had four immediate consequences: Santa Anna's resignation from office as president and the occupation of Mexico City by the North Americans. The new government led by Manuel Peña y Peña began to negotiate a peace with the United States in a series of talks that ended with the signing of the Treaty of Guadalupe Hidalgo in early 1848. Under it, Mexico was obliged to sell Upper California and New Mexico for 15 million dollars; in exchange the United States would pay the costs of the war and cover the damages of its nationals in Mexico.

Santa Anna left the country once more and went into exile in Colombia.

Without any doubt these experiences, combined with the independence of Texas, were frustrating for most Mexicans, who saw that after under thirty years of independence they had lost more than half their territory.

Chapter 5

From the War with the United States to the Second French Intervention (1848 -1864)

Mexico after the War (1848 - 1855)

Once peace had been signed with the United States, Congress appointed José Joaquín Herrera again. This partisan of the conservative party (made up of the former centralists) wanted to heal the wounds left by war by creating a conciliatory government which would work on the rebuilding of the nation and not for a political faction. This was a difficult task because the problems in the country were excessively complicated.

Yucatan had separated from Mexico in 1846 and a year later what is known as the "war of the castes" broke out. This was a mass uprising by the indigenous peoples from the present-day states of Campeche, Quintana Roo and Yucatán against the white population. The movement grew to extraordinary dimensions: the only towns where whites could be safe were Campeche and Mérida, since haciendas were the favorite target of the natives. The reason for this conflict was based on the constant abuses and humiliations inflicted on the different Maya groups by the whites. In the southeast of Mexico it was common for natives to live in a state of slavery, which although prohibited by law, was so brazen that there were still bills of sale for Mayas as slaves.

This situation was insupportable for the white population and therefore in 1848 they asked for Yucatán to be reincorporated into Mexico so that the federal authorities would be responsible for resolving the conflict by sending troops. The president's efforts to put an end to the problem were successful in 1850 when the Indians agreed to lay down their arms and the whites agreed to let them settle on vacant land.

The contributions Herrera made to Mexico also had a social side. He was the first to carry out a campaign against alcoholism, which was rife in rural areas, fought fervently against banditry because he regarded it as a social evil which, in addition to causing insecurity, depleted the domestic economy. He was also concerned about reforming the penitentiary system for prisoners to be treated more humanely and, finally, had more schools and hospitals built because he realized the country's shortage in these areas was holding back its development. This policy was successful to a certain extent but it could have been more so if greater funds had been available.

Herrera was also fortunate enough to complete his administration because —something rare in nineteenth-century Mexican history— no armed uprising or plot removed him from power. In 1851 he was succeeded by Mariano Arista, a moderate liberal, who was also conciliatory and capable.

Things did not go well for Arista. During his term of office the instability which had been quiescent during the previous administration showed itself. The liberals (former federalists) were heading a series of revolts in La Piedad, Michoacán, and Guadalajara which led to the *Plan del Hospicio* in 1851 which repudiated him as president and proposed the return of Santa Anna for the umpteenth time. Although this leader was living in exile in Colombia, he was no doubt the instigator of some of these protests.

The uprisings encouraged an atmosphere of anarchy which, combined with the permanent economic crisis, sank the country into a state of ungovernability that had not existed since before the war with the United States. The situation was so grave that both liberals and conservatives criticized the president and he, seeing he had no support, opted to resign in early 1853 and go into exile in Europe.

The situation was unusual for several reasons. The two opposing parties in fact held the same opinions and made the same criticisms, something which had never occurred before. In addition, the president's resignation was not the result of a military coup but because he was weary of how they both blamed him for the state of the country, but neither of them was helping him to solve the problem. Another unusual feature, perhaps the strangest of all, was that they both believed that the only person who could fill the presidency and so help the country was Santa Anna.

Letters and representatives from both parties reached Colombia to persuade the leader to accept their proposal. This made Santa Anna feel he was indeed indispensable in Mexico and so he decided that not until he arrived would he decide whether to govern with the centralists or the federalists; in short, he would go with the highest bidder.

After landing in Mexico, Santa Anna listened to both the liberal and conservative leaders and decided in favor of the conservatives, This verdict was obviously due to the fact that it was in his interest, since he believed that the conservatives would not limit him in exercising his power, and this would allow him to have better political control of the country.

This presidency, Santa Anna's last term of office, was full of contrasts. It began very well in 1853, as the president showed an adherence to the law such as had rarely been seen from him. and made decisions jointly which were usually the right ones. It seemed to be the beginning of a successful period of administration that would finally rescue the country from crisis; but the prospect suddenly clouded over.

While the conservative leader Lucas Alamán lived, the president conducted himself properly and let himself be "controlled" by the aging politician, but when he died in June, 1853, Santa Anna was no longer restricted and could act freely.

The way Santa Anna accumulated power was subtle and had the help of both liberals and conservatives, who were captivated by the president. The first step toward turning the republican regime into a dictatorship was when Congress granted Santa Anna all-embracing powers, in other words, it yielded its constitutional powers up to him so that he could stabilize the country.

Being given absolute power meant that the leader could manage domestic politics as he pleased and thus establish his dictatorship. He issued a law prohibiting the press from publishing criticisms, however justified, of the government and its members under the pain of imprisonment for editors and writers and the closure of the publication. Magistrates, governors, deputies and other public figures, who began to oppose his arbitrariness were removed from office and imprisoned as an example to all who might wish to follow in their footsteps.

As usually happens in dictatorships, excesses kept increasing until they produced general discontent, which in turn made the dictator more distrustful. Santa Anna's conceit even went as far as to make him feel he was the emperor of Mexico and he demanded to be called Most Serene Highness, used only to refer to monarchs. It was an opportunistic but firm act to reinstate a monarchy in the country. At this time there were many Mexicans who felt frustrated by the federalist and conservative alternatives since neither had given the country the order it needed, and so they upheld the idea of returning to monarchy. Disputes about this centered around the origin of the monarch; some people wanted a foreigner from an important noble house, while others believed it was not necessary to look so far as a Mexican could occupy the throne. The last included Santa Anna's followers. However there were more who opposed this idea, since they were aware of the president's moral qualities; they knew that it would lead the country to ruin.

These were also times of a severe economic crisis or, according to some experts, the worst in Mexico's history, and so Santa Anna took certain "measures" to fight it. By presidential decree, householders had to pay an annual tax on each door and window; carriage owners were taxed, as were the owners of dogs and horses. It would seem to be an economic policy totally without logic, but it was congruent with the regime.

While the situation inside the country grew more and more tense, another war with the United States was on the verge of beginning. This country's government had embarked on the project to build a railroad to connect the Atlantic and Pacific coasts and to reduce expense it would have to run through Mexican territory. The builders pressured their government to help them and it tried to buy the Mesilla Valley between the states of Sonora and Chihuahua, as this was the simplest route. The U.S. government offered Mexico ten million dollars, but the offer was refused as being attempt against national sovereignty. However, when the North Americans suggested that a refusal to sell could cause another war, Santa Anna gave the order for the sale to be made.

In 1854 there was general discontent with Santa Anna all over Mexico. The ones who complained most were the liberals as they saw how a dictatorial regime was taking shape that would lead the country to absolute monarchy, which for them was a synonym for moving backward. They began to plot, but when news of this reached the president's ears he began a campaign of persecution against this political party. Liberals all over the country were imprisoned or assassinated and those who wanted to avoid this fate chose to go into exile. The ordinary people used their imagination and invented a rhyme according to which Mexican liberals could expect *"el encierro, entierro o destierro"* (jail, burial or exile). To prevent his rivals escaping, Santa Anna created a law making passports obligatory to go from one state to another; people who tried to cross borders without the document were to be imprisoned or, if they put up resistance, shot.

But the conservatives were angry too, for although they had brought him to power and were not persecuted, his way of running politics did little to help the country's stability or their economic interests. The difference between the members of this party and the liberals was that they were careful not to show Santa Anna their disagreement.

It would be unfair to say that everything about this administration was bad and that no contributions were made to the nation. The aspect most worthy of note in Santa Anna's last term of office is the creation of the national anthem. The 19th century was the century of nationalism and a fundamental part of this were symbols such as the banners and personal possessions of patriotic heroes. Mexico did not have a national anthem and this, according to the president, was what had caused discord since independence. To solve this problem, he organized a competition in which all the composers and men of letters living in the country to write the words and music of the anthem. There were two winners: the Spaniard Jaime Nunó (music) and the Mexican Francisco González Bocanegra (words).

Bocanegra has been criticized for including Santa Anna and Iturbide in the anthem. These criticisms are unjustified since it must be remembered that the first was responsible for choosing the winner of the contest and in the mid 19th century the second was still considered a national hero by many people. These criticisms grew so strong in the second half of the century that it was decided to eliminate verses IV and VII from the anthem.

More and more Mexicans came to oppose Santa Anna's tyranny, and it was not long before armed rebellions began. The most important of these was the Revolution of Ayutla because of the repercussions it had on the country's history.

The Ayutla Revolution and the War of the Reform (1855 - 1862)

The Ayutla revolution or uprising was organized by s group of liberals led by Juan Álvarez, the most important cacique in the state of Guerrero. They wanted to put an end to Santa Anna's dictatorship, social injustice, social privileges and the country's educational backwardness.

Mexican liberals, both those in the country and those in exile, formed a young generation of politicians with different ideas. Aware of the country's traditional and still smarting from the war with the United States they were ready to do whatever they could to prevent this situation from continuing. Ideologically they can be considered heirs of the most radical aspect of the Progress Party. They firmly believed that the only way to make Mexico a modern country was to make a complete break with the past, which they considered a burden to the nation. Not only were they imitators of the party mentioned above, they also made contributions linked to the liberal ideas that were fashionable in Europe: respect for citizens' rights, the creation of a democratic system, education for the masses and the separation of Church and State.

In the south of the country, especially the state of Guerrero, General Álvarez established a domain *(cacicazgo)* at the beginning of independence. Santa Anna disliked these local political leaders *(caciques)* and Álvarez in particular because of his regional power and clearly liberal ideas. On his part, the chieftain was against the abuses committed by the leader against the members of his party and against the Mexicans in general. Therefore he organized an armed revolt against him.

A group of young and middle-aged liberals joined Juan Álvarez in a rebellion and subscribed to the *Plan de Ayutla*. In this they repudiated Santa Anna and proposed that the army should designate an interim president whose job would be to form a constituent Congress and later, call elections. The movement was successful from the start, especially because it had the support of the liberals exiled in the United States (Benito Juárez, Melchor Ocampo and others), who did not hesitate to share their scarce funds with the survivors. Furthermore, the movement had followers within the country —landowners, military personnel, peasants and merchants decided to take up arms or collaborate in any way they could, until the revolt became nationwide.

In April 1855, Santa Anna took charge of the army and marched on Guerrero with the intention of quashing this hotbed of subversion, but the president showed his lack of military skills once again and was defeated. As the situation was lost, he decided to leave the country before his life was endangered.

The revolutionaries met and, in accordance with the agreements of the Ayutla Plan, proclaimed Juan Álvarez interim president, who in turn called together a Congress.

One important feature of Juan Álvarez' government was that he formed his cabinet of liberals who were all young. It is thanks to this that such important figures in Mexican history as Melchor Ocampo, Benito Juárez, Guillermo Prieto and Ignacio Comonfort had the opportunity of active political participation which in some cases did not end until the late 19th century.

The conservative groups in society, which were not a few, did not support this government because they thought, as in the case of Vicente Guerrero, it was headed by an unskilled politician with little education. At the same time, differences began to surface between the moderates and the hard-liners *(puros)*. In this small "competition" —as it might be called— the first group prevailed, convincing the president it was advisable to maintain the former army and reform it, and also to give members the right to vote.

This administration was interested in passing laws which would help keep the country in order under the ideals of liberalism. Examples of this were the *Ley Juárez* drawn up by Benito Juárez, the minister of justice, which military and ecclesiastical dispensations were suppressed for civil cases, and Melchor Ocampo's legislation taking the right to vote away from the clergy. It was clear that the government was going to apply an aggressive policy against the army and, especially, the clergy, the two groups which identified themselves most closely with the conservative party.

For personal reasons, Juan Álvarez resigned from his position in December 1855 and left the presidency in the hands of Ignacio Comonfort.

Because he was a liberal, Comonfort made it clear that his government would be one of compromise, respectful of liberty and promoter of order. Results did not take long to show; he quickly put down bands of brigands, protesting Indians and initially was able to calm the conservatives down.

However, Comonfort's greatest concern was to create a new Constitution more in tune with liberal ideals. Congress had been sitting since mid 1855, little time to draft a new Constitution. To fill this vacuum the president issued a series of decrees which made much of individual rights (freedom, security, equality and property), abolished slavery, monopolies, degrading punishment, the death penalty and forced loans; prohibited the compulsion of religious vows and the last, which dissolved the Company of Jesus in Mexico once more. Although this was a moderate liberal government, its clear intention was to weaken the Church since it was seen as an organization whose power competed with that of the State.

Seeing these measures the members of Comonfort's cabinet felt freer to act. In 1856 the secretary of the treasury, Miguel Lerdo de Tejada issued the *Ley Lerdo* which demanded the disentailment of civil and ecclesiastical corporations to put inactive wealth into circulation. In other words stipulated that property which although having owners was not used should pass into the hands of the government to be sold. Basically, the purpose was to weaken the economic power of the clergy, create a group of small landholders and increase State revenues.

This same year the *Ley Iglesias* was issued which prohibited the Church from charging the poor tithes and rights.

Finally the Constitution was proclaimed on February 5, 1857 —and this is why it is known as the Constitution of 1857. Debates among the liberals were heated. The radicals, although a minority, had a star representative in Valentín Gómez Farías, who was bent on having the principles of the Progress Party included in the new Constitution. For their part, the moderates wanted the liberal principles in the document but did not wish all the principles of this party to be incorporated since their virulence might cause disorder. It was due to the constant arguments and the absence of any consensus that the Constitution did not see light soon.

This document defined Mexico as "republican, federalist, democratic and liberal" and showed greater concern for social issues, especially individual rights. In accordance with liberal thought, it recognized that people had certain rights by birth, not by the will of the State, and that these should be respected by political authorities and institutions. Article three referred to the freedom of education, four to the freedom of work, seven dealt with the freedom of the press, while number five recognized the right to receive a fair daily wage and stated that monastic vows went against human freedom. In the matter of religion, Articles 15 and 127 were the ones which caused most arguments, since while the first recognized the freedom of worship, though giving preference to Roman Catholicism, the second gave the State right to legislate on religious issues. As regards respect for the rights of individuals, this Constitution made a great contribution by incorporating the law on the right to *amparo* designed to defend citizens against abuse by the State.

At first criticisms and speeches were made by both conservatives and liberals, but as tempers grew heated the two factions exchanged the pen for the sword.

In the same year, conservative movements against the government emerged. These were intended to bring down the president and remove the liberal laws. Of all the uprisings, the Puebla one was the strongest. In it, the military and the clergy united to take over the city, turn it into the center of the movement and put an end to the liberal laws. After much effort, Comonfort managed to take the city and ordered a series of drastic measures to serve as a lesson to the other rebels in the country. Church goods were confiscated, while the rebellious members of the clergy and the military were either imprisoned, shot or sent into exile.

Revolts continued and began to spread through the country, so that the struggle between the government, clergy and army became a civil war.

General Félix Zuloaga, a dyed-in-the-wool conservative, launched the *Plan de Tacubaya* in which he repudiated the Constitution of 1857, proposed the creation of a new constituent Congress and recognized Comonfort as the president of the country with all-embracing powers so that he would join the movement and it would have more chance of success. The president chose to join the rebels because he thought that state authorities and most of the liberal group would follow him, which actually never happened. His fellow party members did not agree that the Reform Laws should be repealed and even less when the president, under the influence of the conservatives, had had Benito Juárez —at this time chief justice of the Supreme Court— imprisoned. It was this last act that showed the liberals that Félix Zuloaga was the one who really governed the country.

The liberals' lack of support for the president displeased the conservatives who, seeing that although still in office he was no longer useful to them, decided to remove him from his position. In January 1858, the garrisons of Mexico City and Tacubaya rejected the president and declared themselves in favor of Zuloaga. Comonfort recognized his mistake and to make amends for it now that he was not in power released Benito Juárez and other liberals from prison, agreed on an armistice with Zuloaga and went into exile in the United States.

Juárez did not remain in the capital since he knew he was in danger but fled to safety in Guanajuato. He declared he was the rightful president of Mexico by reason of his position of chief justice of the Supreme Court. Although it was legitimate, the announcement had little effect because most of the army and its great leaders had gone over to the conservatives, while those who followed him were mostly civilians and some career military men.

When things went against him, Juárez had to leave Guanajuato and take refuge in Guadalajara, where traitors from his own army took him prisoner and intended to execute him. However, the statesman from Oaxaca was spared thanks to the intervention of Guillermo Prieto who gave a speech which persuaded the proposed executioners not to make this mistake. From Manzanillo, Juárez left for Veracruz where he arrived in May 1858 and there established his government.

The conservative advance was swift and this made them feel they were masters of the republic and victors of the war, since almost a year after beginning, the fight was going in their favor. However, in 1858 when disagreements began to emerge among the members of the group, a contingent of conservative soldiers repudiated Zuloaga and proclaimed General Miguel Miramón president of Mexico.

Miramón was a young army man, one of the most brilliant in Mexico's history according to some military historians, who was famed for being very successful in the matter of arms. Two details about this figure are worth pointing out: he studied in the Military Academy at the same time as the "Boy heroes" and was the youngest president in the history of Mexico, being only 26 years old when he took up office.

Miramón was proclaimed president in February 1859 and as a first step decided to take the port of Veracruz to finish Juárez and the war. Despite the superior numbers of his army, the president was not able to take the port and had to be satisfied with laying siege to it. Meanwhile, the liberal general Degollado sallied out of Toluca to attack Mexico City but was defeated by the conservative Leonardo Márquez.

The year 1859 was an important one because the forces engaged in the war were evenly matched and this so bogged down the fighting that no clear end was in sight. Juárez nevertheless continued his work and, believing the time had come to hit the allies of the conservatives hard, decreed the *Reform Laws*.

These laws were intended to put the liberal philosophy of Ayutla into practice. During the armed struggle, his main aim was to attack the Church because it was an institution which vied with the power of the State and impeded the full development of both it and Mexican society.

Another result of this stalemate was the wish of both sides to obtain recognition from abroad. And therefore both liberals and conservatives began to seek allies outside the country. Juárez obtained recognition from the United States and Miramón from Spain. The two nations became involved in the conflict to gain from it, so they both signed treaties in which they each laid down certain conditions in return for recognition.

The liberals signed the *McLane-Ocampo Treaty* with the United States, so called for the two persons involved in it; Melchor Ocampo for Mexico and Robert McLane for the United States. Under it the United States recognized Benito Juárez as president of Mexico in exchange for the concession in perpetuity to the right of traffic across the isthmus of Tehuantepec and the seaway between the ports of Mazatlán and Guaymas in the case of U.S. citizens. In addition it demanded that

American troops be permitted free entry from Guaymas to Nogales. This document caused considerable criticism from the moderate liberals since they would have preferred to sign a peace treaty with the conservatives rather than "sell" the country to the United States as they said Juárez was doing. But the treaty was rejected by the U.S. senate.

The conservatives signed the *Mon-Almonte Treaty* in which Spain imposed two conditions for recognizing Miramón as president; that Mexico should pay compensation to the relatives of the Spaniards killed on the haciendas of San Vicente, Chiconcuac and San Dimas; it also demanded Mexico's recognition of its debt to Spain —almost 2,500,000 pesos.

In 1860 the conservative president tried to take Veracruz for the second time. He thought he should add a sea blockade to the siege on land. The maritime action was a complete failure; his ships were attacked by U.S. vessels that by the request of Juárez were lying off the port city.

The move was such a huge failure that Miramón proposed peace to Juárez because he thought it was the only way to end the conflict, but the liberal president turned down the offer because he realized that to accept would mean that he recognized he was not president and that the balance of the war was shifting to Miramón's side.

To finance the end of the war the liberals seized Church silver and one million pesos were taken from private citizens. Meanwhile Miramón in a rash move prompted by the urgent need to raise funds negotiated with the Swiss banker J.B. Jecker for a loan of just over 700 thousand pesos in return for which the conservative government would pay 15 million.

At the end of 1860 the liberals were at the gates of Mexico City. Miramón went out to fight them but was soundly defeated by General Jesús González Ortega at San Miguel Calpulalpan in the State of Mexico on December 22, 1860, and as a result he fled abroad. The liberals entered Mexico City on December 25, 1860, so putting an end to three years of civil war.

The war had ended, but not the instability. The Juárez government still had to face up to groups of conservatives waging guerrilla warfare in the hope of obtaining foreign help, but without any success.

Juárez reinstated Congress for it to proclaim him president and for constitutional order to hold sway again. Following this he expelled Mexicans —whether they were bishops, illustrious army commanders or outstanding politicians— and foreigners who had supported his rivals during the war. This measure caused unrest among the conservatives, especially those who were still in revolt, as they considered it a hostile act of the government's against them. In revenge a band of conservative partisans captured Ocampo, the great friend and close collaborator of Benito Juárez, and had him shot in 1861.

The times following the war were difficult for Juárez because although he had been ratified in the office of president by Congress, there was some unease about him in the country. The press criticized that after the war neither he nor his cabinet had been able to pacify Mexico; it also accused him of not having complied with the Constitution of 1857 because during the War of the Reform and the first months of 1861 he had governed "at his whim," in other words autocratically.

Tempers were so inflamed that the Congress, in an attempt to calm them and begin the process of rebuilding the country, proposed that Juárez should continue in office. The debates between the president's detractors and defenders were very heated. In a vote, 51 of the 103 members of Congress demanded his removal, and 52 his continuance. This was what gave Juárez the opportunity to continue as president.

Another great problem for the Juárez administration was the economy. After the War of the Reform the liberal government found itself bankrupt. The disastrous aftermath of the war contributed to this, but so did the liberals' exaggerated estimate of the value of Church property, some of which had been sold off at ridiculously low prices, and the inability of different ministers of the treasury to put government accounts in order.

The situation was serious because with the economy in such a sorry state and in considerable debt it was impossible to set about rebuilding and modernizing the country. As money was in short supply the government was faced with a choice between beginning to pay off the country's foreign debts or investing the available funds in Mexico. Juárez opted for the second alternative and declared a moratorium with the phrase "Survive, then pay". The countries most affected were England, owed 70,000,000 pesos, Spain 9,500,00, and France 3,000,000.

This decision offended these countries, not so much in itself as the way it was applied: Mexico, the debtor nation, had decided unilaterally not to meet the obligations it had held for a long time. In reprisal, England, France and Spain broke off diplomatic relations with it.

In October 1861, representatives of these three countries met in London with the idea of forming a common front to demand payment from the Mexican government. There they agreed to send their armies to Veracruz and also declared that they would not go inland for any reason and would not interfere in Mexico's internal affairs. England and Spain were prepared to abide by this agreement —known as the Convention of London— but France had other ideas.

The Second French Intervention (1862 - 1864)

The emperor of France, Napoieon III, wanted to establish an empire in America that would unite all the Latin peoples and halt the advance of Anglo-Saxon Americans. To give this project an ideological basis he coined the term "Latin American". Latin America included, and still does, all the lands on the American continent with Romance languages and cultures. France, as a country with a Latin heritage supposedly had kinship with them.

In December 1861 and January 1862 the Spanish, English and French (in this order) reached Veracruz. When the three armies disembarked in Mexico their commanders demanded the payment of debts. Juárez tried to solve the problem by diplomatic means, sending a message to the representatives of the three countries saying that his government did not disavow the debt and inviting them to talk about how to clear up the situation. Shortly afterward, the envoys of Juárez's government and the representative of the Europeans met. The talks went well and on February 19 the preliminary agreements were signed, called the La Soledad agreements for the small town where this took place. In a gesture of good will the Mexican government allowed the foreign troops to establish themselves in Orizaba and Tehuacán, towns with a healthier climate than the port.

It did not take the French long to show what their real intentions were. The French representative was intolerant toward the Mexican government, an attitude which grew worse when in March the Duke of Lorençez reached Mexico at the head of more than 4,000 troops, in an act that was hardly friendly or diplomatic.

There is a curious fact connected with this. Various conservatives arrived with Lorençez. Among them Juan Nepomuceno Almonte, the son of José María Morelos y Pavón, the rebel leader who had fought in the War of Independence.

The arrival of more French soldiers broke the atmosphere of calm surrounding the negotiations since the son of Morelos began to incite the people of Veracruz to rebel against Juárez' government, who in turn broke all contact with the French. Spain and England saw that France had violated what had been agreed at the Convention of London, so both nations broke the alliance, negotiated separately with Mexico and sailed their troops out.

Faced with the possibility of an armed struggle against France, Juárez realized that he had scant funds. He signed the *Corwin-Doblado Treaty* with the American government for a loan of 11 million dollars payable in six years. Under it, Mexico had to pledge Baja California, Chihuahua, Sonora and Sinaloa as guarantee. The treaty never came into effect since the American Congress was not able to ratify it because the War of Secession broke out.

In April 1862, the French army began hostilities against the Mexican army and government. After a series of easy victories in Veracruz the Europeans marched toward the city of Puebla, a conservative, proclerical city which was being defended by the liberal general Ignacio Zaragoza.

The battle for Puebla began on May 5 and, thanks to the clever tactics of Zaragoza, the Mexican troops managed to defeat the French army, then the most prestigious in the world. This victory raised the morale of the Mexican troops and government.

In late 1862, more than 30,000 French reinforcements landed at Veracruz under the command of marshals Frédéric Forey and Achille Bazaine.

Juárez and other sensible politicians realized that the war was not yet over, so the president decided to take certain measures to ensure the continuing defense of the country; all Mexicans who collaborated with the invaders would be executed without trial; males between the ages of 16 and 70 who lived in the important cities were obliged to work one day per week on fortifications. On March 16, 1863, the French attacked Puebla again; its former defender, General Ignacio Zaragoza had died of typhoid in 1862 and now the invading army did manage to take the city after a cruel siege which lasted sixty-two days. This opened the doors to the capital.

On their way to Mexico City the French received help from conservative troops and this, together with the fall of Puebla, enabled them to advance so rapidly that after occupying the capital they could take the most important cities of the center in a short time.

Juárez decided to leave Mexico City and move north, thus beginning a journey which would take him to Saltillo, Monterrey and Paso del Norte (now Ciudad Juárez). The Juarist government experienced hard times during this period since it was decimated by the different persecutions it suffered and by the desertion of followers of the regime. Others asked Juárez to resign from the presidency and, to top everything, there were not enough weapons because the North American president refused to sell any.

The French victory encouraged the reappearance of projects among certain conservatives, who explained the failure of the first attempt at monarchy in Mexico by the fact that Iturbide had been an opportunist without any royal blood, two defects that prevented him from having the respectability of a true sovereign. Monarchism was not new. Since the 1840s, a group of monarchists had been traveling around Europe in search of help to give Mexico a new monarch, The leading figures of this group were José María Gutiérrez Estrada and José Manuel Hidalgo, famous because they were the ones to make contact with Napoleon III.

When the French reached the capital they organized fortifications on the outskirts of the city in case Juárez decided to attack, established courts martial to try opponents of the intervention and tranquilized the purchasers of Church property by assuring them that by order of Napoleon III the *Ley Lerdo* would not be repealed.

To comply with the instructions of the French emperor, Forey selected a provisional government made up of conservative politicians, army men and clerics. He also created an Assembly of Notables to choose the type of government the country was to have. This was a pre-arranged plan because, as has been seen, Napoleon III wanted Mexico to be an empire, but he did not wish to be seen by Mexicans as the one who imposed an emperor on them. This is why when Forey created this Council he chose mostly monarchists to be its members.

As was to be expected, the Assembly of Notables decided that the government would be a monarchy that was moderate, hereditary with a Catholic sovereign; that he would be given the title of Emperor of Mexico; that the imperial crown should be offered (at Napoleon's "suggestion") to Prince Ferdinand Maximilian, archduke of Austria, and that if he were unable —or unwilling— to accept the crown, the French emperor would be asked to choose another Catholic prince. Once this had been decided, the Assembly sent an embassy to Europe to offer Maximilian the throne of Mexico.

The liberal policy that the French applied in Mexico caused trouble. General Bazaine and Pelagio Antonio de Labastida y Dávalos, archbishop of Mexico City were not on good terms and serious problems arose between them. The general respected the legislation of Juárez, while the cleric insisted that such a decision should be taken by the future emperor and until then the Reform Laws should be suspended. The archbishop threatened to close all the churches in the city, and the general in turn threatened to reopen them with cannon fire. Finally, none of this happened and there was no change whatsoever in the law.

On the military front, guerilla bands sprang up all over the country which fought the French troops tenaciously.

Chapter 6

The Second Empire and the Restored Republic (1864 - 1877)

The Second Empire (1864 - 1867)

In 1863, the Mexican delegation sent by the Assembly of Notables arrived at the Palace of Miramar near Trieste, Italy, to make Maximilian of Hapsburg, brother of Franz Joseph, Emperor of Austria, the formal offer of the throne of Mexico. The delegates went to Italy because it was still not unified and Austria occupied the northern part, which at the time was governed by Maximilian. The delegates were welcomed warmly by the Austrian aristocrat, who showed some reserve when he was given the invitation. The reason was not that he disliked the idea of going to Mexico but because a short time before, the Greeks had also offered him the throne of their country. He thought deeply about things for some time and finally accepted the responsibility of ruling the American country. It is a fact that the Austrian's acceptance was due to the fact that he preferred to rule on the American continent —he had visited Brazil earlier— since he thought he would have a better future there. He firmly believed that this "adventure" would be a success thanks to French support and also that his mission was praiseworthy: to establish a government in Mexico that would save it from chaos and draw it into the modern world.

Maximilian wanted to be sure that the Mexicans would accept him as emperor so he placed as a condition on agreeing that the delegation

Emperor
Maximiliano of
Habsburgo.

at Miramar show him the Mexicans' documents of accession. When he
received these in February 1864 he agreed to rule the country.

Before sailing for Mexico, Maximilian went to Austria where his
brother Franz Joseph made him renounce all rights to the throne of
Austria. After this, he signed the Convention of Miramar with Napoleon
III. This established that there would be French troops in Mexico to
give the emperor military support for six years, that preferential
treatment would be given to French officials over Mexicans, and that
military power would remain in the hands of a French commandant.
In economic matters, Maximilian recognized a debt of 54 million pesos, pledged to pay 1,000 francs a year for every French soldier in Mexico
and to compensate all the French citizens affected by the War of
Intervention.

Maximilian wanted the support of other European nations, but only
the pope was ready to help him. He had an interview with Pius X in
Rome, who made a condition of his help the suppression of the *Reform
Laws*. The emperor of Mexico agreed to the condition even though he

was against it since he felt that what Juárez had done in religious matters was correct.

When all the necessary arrangements had been made, the emperor and his wife, the Belgian princess Charlotte Amélie (henceforth in Mexico to be known as Carlota) sailed for Mexico on an Austrian ship. During the voyage, Maximilian thought deeply how he could fight the instability of his empire, in particular the problem of the Juarist military uprising. As he believed the best way was through dialogue, he thought of writing Juárez a letter inviting him to be part of his government.

The imperial couple reached Veracruz in May 1864. The inhabitants of the port gave them a cold welcome and only a few members of the provisional government were there to meet them. However, as they approached the capital, he situation changed, and public demonstrations of support and recognition became more frequent. When they reached Mexico City they had a magnificent welcome and triumphal arches, pavilions and columns were set up all over the city in honor of Maximilian and Carlota.

A few days after arriving in the capital, the emperor formed his cabinet. He included both moderate conservatives and liberals because by doing this he hoped to show his interest in ruling for all Mexicans. He also created a cabinet he could trust composed of foreign liberals which supported his plans not to give in to pressure from the Church and the most conservative groups.

Maximilian was to a certain extent an agitator, because while he might not have told the conservative groups that he disagreed with them, he did show them this with acts that were obviously bound to annoy them. He refused to include the cross in the imperial coat of arms, neither did he want to sign with the phrase "By the Grace of God;" he gave audiences to the city's poor on Sundays; he publicly praised the liberal general Ignacio Zaragoza, and placed statues of Morelos and Guerrero throughout the city when he discovered that the Mexican upper classes were declaring themselves Iturbidist.

Actions like these showed that the emperor was a liberal and therefore wanted to attract members of this group to his cause. As a gesture of goodwill, he offered them an amnesty and sent the conservative general Miguel Miramón to Prussia as Mexico's ambassador in what was in fact exile in disguise.

The radical liberals did not accept these offers since they came from an unlawful foreign government which had removed the legitimate government of Mexico, i.e. Juárez, from office. For them, the situation was far from easy since persecutions, lack of arms and desertions forced them to lead a wandering life. So it was not unusual to see a black carriage racing through the country. This was Juárez's coach (now displayed in the museum of Chapultepec Castle) and for many people it was the seat of the legitimate government of Mexico.

The picture seemed to clear a little when the American Civil War ended in 1865. However, the question was not so simple since the victorious U.S. government was not prepared to help Juárez without gaining some benefit from the situation. The American negotiators managed to get a treaty signed which allowed the U.S.A. to settle land in Baja California and gave them concessions to build the El Paso —Guaymas and Matamoros— Mazatlán railroads.

Juárez's problems continued when in December 1865 he decided to extend his constitutional term of office. The decision gave rise to divisions, since while the president justified it by pointing out that there was no Congress he could summon to endorse the election, his detractors categorically opposed the decision as unconstitutional. Reasons of State and legitimacy were in dispute and the first won, so Juárez continued as the country's executive power.

While the war went on, Maximilian was working to establish a real government in Mexico that would enable it to grow and consolidate as a power in Latin America first and then on a world scale. At this time the emperor had more than 60,000 soldiers at his disposal to support the throne; half were foreign and half Mexican. Urged by the French military leader Bazaine, in October Maximilian signed a law under which all opponents of the empire still carrying arms were to be shot. This law was applied immediately and several leading liberal officers were executed.

As his empire still did not have a Constitution but had to be governed by laws to avoid the problems which occurred during Iturbide's administration, in 1865 he enacted the Provisional Statute of the Mexican Empire, a document of liberal persuasion which gave a favored place to issues such as individual rights and the freedom of worship.

As regards the Indians, the imperial couple showed a philanthropic spirit, hoping to improve the living conditions of ethnic groups, but without making structural changes. The emperor promulgated a series of laws designed to make the life of Indian peasants less hard, since they ordered the abolition of corporal punishment, the limitation of working hours, the abolition of *tiendas de raya* (company stores) and payment in kind, prohibited the *leva* (forced conscription) and decreed the distribution of uncultivated land to peasants who had no property. Unfortunately, these did not prevent the ills they sought to remedy from continuing.

The monarchs also occupied themselves with beautifying the city because it did not have the appearance of what was to be the capital of such a great empire as Mexico. They not only adorned it with statues, parks and gardens but also changed its face by having the *Paseo del Emperador* (today Paseo de la Reforma) built, a wide avenue running from Chapultepec Castle to the city center. Perhaps the building which best represents this epoch is Chapultepec Castle, which was the imperial residence. This was erected over what had been a small country house of the viceroys and later the Military Academy. Although the building was inhabited by the monarchs for only a short time, the richness of its construction and decoration, as well as its size, make it one of the most attractive architectural monuments in Mexico.

To an extent, the emperors relations with the Church were never good because it did not matter to Maximilian. However, as a result of the visit Pius IX had made years earlier, at the end of December 1864 the pope sent Monsignor Meglia to Mexico whose instructions were very clear and specific: to help repeal the *Reform Laws*, ensure the return of all the goods taken from the Church, make the State recognize the right of the Church to hold property and respect its autonomy. The purpose of all this was to make it possible for The Holy See and Mexico to formalize their relations. The emperor, on his own convictions, had decided to respect the decrees on the disentailment and nationalization of Church property issued by Juárez, because he believed it necessary to submit the Church to the State in order to consolidate his empire.

When the pope's envoy and the emperor met, these differences came to the surface and as Maximilian did not want to lose the pope's support, but did not want to yield to his pressure either, he presented Meglia with the plan for a concordat which was to guide relations between civil and religious power.

The document was unacceptable to the Church because under it the government gained everything and the clergy lost all. Meglia refused to sign. Maximilian, through fear of having lost the Vatican's support, sent a delegation to persuade the pope to accept. The latter rejected it as being inadmissible as the foundation for relations between Church and State. Immediately after this he withdrew Meglia from Mexico and broke off relations with the country.

Things were not going well in economic affairs either. Napoleon made French officials responsible for finding an answer to Mexico's financial situation, but they failed to do so; if in times of peace it had not been possible to generate the wealth to guarantee the country's self-sufficiency, in wartime the situation was even more critical. Maximilian finally had to resort to incurring foreign debt. Two loans were requested from France for a total of 46 million pesos, of which only 16 million were granted. Despite the injection of these funds, the empire's deficit did not diminish and continued to be an obstacle to the country's development. Maximilian held the French army responsible for this, alleging that its expenses were excessive, but in turn, the military leaders blamed the emperor because he liked to spend funds on such trivialities as palaces, streets, statues and theaters. It is a fact that this chronic economic crisis experienced by the Second Empire can be considered as one of the factors that caused it to disappear.

Maximilian's position deteriorated considerably in 1867. For a start, he lost French support. In January an envoy from Napoleon III met him to inform him of the emperor's intentions: to arrange for the withdrawal of French troops from Mexico. The French leader was violating the agreement made with the emperor of Mexico because a war against Prussia was imminent and he wanted to be prepared. It was a great blow that Maximilian had never expected to receive from the person who was the only solid military support of his empire. He though of abdicating but his wife, the Empress Carlota, resolved to go to Paris to persuade Napoleon to continue upholding the Mexican throne, but her efforts were in vain.

After losing French military support the emperor sought help elsewhere. His brother-in-law the king of Belgium, showed no interest in helping him; his brother wanted to send troops but pressure from the United States stopped him. Maximilian sent Carlota to Pope Pius IX to see if she could obtain his support (which would oblige other Catholic countries to help him). After failing in all her efforts, Carlota suffered several fits of insanity from which she never recovered.

Faced with this, Maximilian tried to come close to the conservatives. He put his liberal thinking to one side and repealed some anticlerical laws. With this he only succeeded in falling into the hands of the most radical conservatives, who twice prevented him from abdicating and leaving the country.

Meanwhile, Benito Juárez continued the fight and was supported by the troops which had demonstrated their loyalty to him during the War of the Reform. Thanks to a loan from the U.S.A. of 20 million dollars Juárez was able to form well-trained regular armies, one of whose leaders was Porfirio Díaz, who had performed outstandingly in the siege of Puebla. The injection of fresh funds and the reorganization of the army were factors which gave republican troops a notable superiority over the imperial forces. Within a short time the liberals were recovering the areas lost in the center and south of the country, from which the French gradually retreated.

As a last resort, Maximilian put himself at the head of his troops commanded by Generals Méndez, Miramón and Mejía and headed for the city of Querétaro, which because of its geographical location was easier to defend than Mexico City, to begin the last, decisive battle against his enemies. The emperor reached Querétaro in February, 1867. During March and April surrounded the city and finally, after a 60-day siege, took it. On May 15 Maximilian and his generals Mejía and Miramón surrendered to the Juarist troops commanded by General Mariano Escobedo.

The law applied to them was the one issued by Juárez at the time of the Second French Intervention which laid down that all those who collaborated with the enemy would be executed. The first to be shot was General Méndez and, after all attempts to save their lives had failed, the other three were executed on the Cerro de las Campanas on June 19. Maximilian's body was sent to Vienna shortly afterward on the same ship that had originally carried him to Mexico.

Famous men of such stature as Giuseppe Garibaldi and Victor Hugo, powers such as the United States, England and France pleaded clemency for Maximilian but Juárez was unswerving and made it clear to the world that Mexico was determined to maintain its independence. Juárez announced "The government has never before wished to or had to let itself be swayed by any feeling of anger against those who have fought against it, and it should not now in the Republic's hour of triumph. The government has demonstrated its wish to moderate strict justice as far as possible, reconciling leniency with the duty to ensure that laws are applied in whatever is essential for guaranteeing the nation's peace and future."

After years of absence, the federal army led by Porfirio Díaz made its entry into Mexico City on June 21, 1867. Three weeks later Benito Juárez, president of the Mexican Republic, was to do the same.

The Restored Republic (1867 - 1877)

The triumph of republican ideas over monarchic ones, combined with Juárez's continuity in power were factors which promoted the definitive reinstatement of the republic in Mexico. The fact of having solved the

Benito Juárez.

problem of the form of government gave later administrations, for the first time since independence, a blueprint which included political, social, cultural and economic issues.

When Juárez took up power again, the first thing he did was to inform his companions at arms and fellow party members of the program that he and his successors would have to implement to build a different Mexico, one on the right road to modernity. The proposals of this program were: in politics, the strict application of the *Constitution of 1857*, the strengthening of federalism and the reduction of the army. In the social field, efforts were to be made to encourage immigration, primarily from Europe, small-holdings and the respect for individual rights. As for the economy, there was talk of attracting foreign capital, completing the Mexico City —Veracruz railroad, encouraging industrial growth and introducing new farming techniques. Proposals as regards culture were to provide education for all Mexicans, foster nationalism in letters and the arts and at the same time combat Indianism as being an obstacle to the nation's growth.

105

These proposals drawn up by Juárez were very encouraging, and more so if the situation prevailing in the country is taken into account. Hordes of bandits and conservative guerillas haunted the roads and cities; there was no free movement of either goods or travelers over the Mexico City —Veracruz route; disputes flared up among the liberals, now between two different lines of thought: antimilitarist and militarist. Juárez belonged to the first category; he did not trust military personnel for being extremely ambitious, and on their part the army men doubted the ability of civilians to govern and believed they would not recompense them for their efforts against Maximilian.

Their fears were not completely ungrounded, since in one of his first decrees Juárez ordered the army reduced by 75%. He justified this measure by that in this way expenditure would be reduced and the funds saved could be allocated to other budget items, but fundamentally it was a measure to take power away from the army and subdue the soldiers who had shown most independence from the government.

Complaints from the army were quick to arrive and to confront the situation Juárez adopted a conciliatory policy, later followed by Porfirio Díaz; high-ranking officers were swamped with honors, decorations and privileges in an attempt to mollify them, while those who demonstrated their unconformity publicly were severely repressed.

A fundamental change that Juárez made to democratize the country's political life was the electoral reform of 1867, with sights on the elections that were to be held in December that year. Under it, males aged over 25, whether property owners or not, could vote directly for the president, members of Congress and Supreme Court judges.

He also made reforms to the Constitution before the elections designed to strengthen the existing political institutions, regulate the functions of the different powers and give more authority to the executive. This last point was, according to Juárez, essential in order to be able to govern the country, because only with a strong president would it be possible to achieve the centralization of power necessary for bringing order to the country.

In keeping with this stance, Juárez created the Senate, responsible for declaring the constitutional powers of the states null and void, appointing provisional governors and resolve political disputes among state powers if one of the parties involved should request such assistance.

Juárez also worked for the economic and material progress of the country, trying to reduce foreign debt by imposing tighter financial control.

This was also the time when more highways and ports began to be built to revitalize the country's economic life and stimulate foreign trade. During the presidency of Juárez and Lerdo de Tejada, impetus was given to the ports of Mazatlán, San Blas, Manzanillo, Acapulco, Zihuatanejo, Puerto Ángel, Veracruz and Matamoros.

As for the countryside, Juárez's idea was to create a large rural middle class, copying North American farmers, which would be independent and put an end to subsistence farming. The plan failed because although the authorities began to sell the lands taken from the Church, they fell into the hands of large landowners, who took advantage of the opportunity to increase the extent of their estates and so shatter the dream of a rural middle class.

In education, history and literature took on great importance. They became the ideal means to foster national pride in the young. Literature, of the *costumbrista* school, told what life was like for the different social groups of the country (the rich, the urban poor, the rural poor, etc.) in an attempt to discover what the essence of Mexico was.

Despite the serious economic hardships, the regime's educational policy had some successes, such as the creation of the National Preparatory School and the appearance of mixed schools, which gave girls the opportunity to study.

This was Juárez's presidency. When it ended in 1871, two candidates for the office of president were the most talked about: General Porfirio Díaz and Sebastián Lerdo de Tejada; however, Juárez also soon made public his intention to run for reelection. His candidacy surprised many because it was in violation of the Constitution of 1857, but Juárez justified himself saying that four years was too short a time to put his national plan into practice.

Lerdo de Tejada, Secretary of Foreign Relations and chief justice of the Supreme Court, had carried out an electoral campaign among the civilians who had fallen out with Juárez years earlier and had persuaded the president to put friends of his in important political positions. Porfirio Díaz represented the military resentful of Juárez because of his antimilitarist and centralist policy, and at the same time, a generation of young liberals who thought it was time to renew the ruling political class.

The elections were held in June 1871 in a tense climate caused by the constant irregularities and acts of violence that occurred during the process. Juárez won, with Díaz and Lerdo in second and third place respectively.

The rumor that fraud had been committed against Díaz spread quickly among the army and it did not take long for some officers loyal to him to revolt in the center and north of the country, while in Oaxaca Diaz himself proclaimed the *Plan de la Noria* and rose in arms. This plan criticized Juárez as a dictator, repudiated him as the country's legitimate authority and advocated more respect for citizens' rights.

The revolt never had mass support either from the army or civilians, and it did not spread through the country. What put an end to it was the death of Juárez in July 1872, because once the president was dead, the revolt lost its raison d'être. The person who benefited was Lerdo de Tejada because as chief justice of the Supreme Court he became the interim president.

To calm the situation in which the country found itself, he declared an amnesty for all those who had revolted, pardoning their lives and restoring their political rights. This was how the interim president put an end to the Porfirist uprising and, consequently, Díaz had to submit himself to the government, but that did not mean that his political ambitions diminished.

Lerdo de Tejada then had to call presidential elections, in accordance with the constitution, which would be held in 1872. The circumstances in which they took place were similar to those of the previous elections since there was both fraud and violence. The results were those expected: Lerdo won 20 times more votes than the general. Díaz considered that he had been robbed, but never expressed this publicly and never considered organizing another revolt because he was sure this would fail miserably: after the amnesty, no soldier would follow him.

Lerdo's presidency was little different from that of Juárez. He kept the Juarist cabinet, continued centralizing power in the figure of the executive, promoted education and the immigration policy (which still had no success), followed the same economic program (building railroads and the telegraph system) and suffered the same failures (attraction of foreign capital and the growth of large estates). At first sight, the relationship between the two presidents would seem so close that they had no differences even in political matters.

Perhaps there were two main differences between Juárez and Lerdo: the way the second exercised power and his stance regarding the Church. Lerdo never worried about pretending that his government was democratic; from the start he showed the signs of a dictator such as the imposition of candidates, arbitrary removal of public officials, the systematic violation of laws, etc. As regards the Church, in his last years of government, Juárez was tolerant, so much so that he even gave back its members the right to vote. Lerdo on the other hand toughened the government's stance on religious issues from the beginning of his administration, sending Congress a bill ordering the expulsion of the Jesuits from Mexico. This move caused disgust among prelates as it was clear State aggression against the Church. However, this was only the beginning of an anticlerical policy which would culminate in a decree raising the *Reform Laws* to the level of constitutional.

The last months of Lerdo's administration were very unstable —Liberal and conservative uprisings alternated, all with the same aim: to topple the president. Lerdo was not worried because he knew that as long as the army was on his side —which had been the case so far—

all these violent shows of dissatisfaction would not triumph. And so it was.

Lerdo's opponents saw a natural leader in Porfirio Díaz who, if he so made up his mind, could lead a revolt against the president. For his part, Díaz did not hide his aspirations to the presidency and waited for the right moment to lead Lerdo's critics.

In January, 1876, a few days after Lerdo had made public his intentions to run for a second term of office, Porfirio Díaz did not turn a deaf ear to public discontent and revolted with the *Plan de Tuxtepec*. This repudiated Lerdo's government and all the officials loyal to him; José María Iglesias was named interim president because he was chief justice of the Supreme Court, and it was proposed to respect the Constitution of 1857, especially in regard to no-reelection.

Díaz marched toward Tamaulipas to begin the rebellion proclaiming a manifesto establishing no-reelection, but he and his men were defeated by government troops. From Veracruz he marched back to Oaxaca.

As was to be expected, the Tuxtepec revolution was a success in that it led to other local uprisings that gave the revolt a nationwide character. This did not matter to Lerdo who after an electoral process of very doubtful legality was ratified by Congress as president for the period 1876 - 1880. José María Iglesias did not accept the legitimacy of the election or of the president and in October published a manifesto in which he appointed himself interim president, pointing out that he was chief justice of the Supreme Court.

When Lerdo finally realized the gravity of the situation he could do little to rectify it favorably. The troops who did not support Díaz had proclaimed themselves for Iglesias and only a few remained faithful to the president. Although his friends advised him to renounce his position and go into exile, Lerdo refused because this could be seen as implying recognition of his illegitimate position, and chose to take up arms against his enemies. In November 1876 the armies of Díaz and Lerdo met on the hacienda of Tecoac, Tlaxcala, and after a bloody battle the first emerged victorious. Lerdo had no option but to resign and go into exile in the United States.

Iglesias first applauded the triumph, but when he realized that Díaz would not give up until he attained the presidency, he tried to put up resistance to him. Díaz knew that his rival's troops were very limited in number and began talks with him and convinced him that it would be better to lay down arms because he had no way of defeating him since only a minor part of the army was on his side. Iglesias understood the situation and in early 1877 resigned from the Supreme Court and left the country accompanied by a few supporters, who included General Mariano Escobedo.

Then, the interim president, Juan Méndez —imposed by Díaz— proceeded to call elections, elections cleaner than the earlier ones which ended in an overwhelming victory for Díaz, who was elected president for the period 1877 - 1880.

Chapter 7

The Porfiriato (1877 - 1910)

The Beginnings (1877 - 1888)

The ascent of General Porfirio Díaz to the presidency was similar to that of other presidents in that after a bloody struggle to gain the post, once in it he had to face serious problems.

In his first term of office Díaz could do little to govern. Lacking political experience and strong allies in civilian society the general had no time to concern himself with the social, economic and cultural development of the country. He did what he had always done: depend on the army's help to control rebels and begin to centralize power. The first test came in 1878 when General Escobedo returned to Mexico, intending to proclaim Lerdo president. He was defeated then set free by order of Díaz.

Although the general believed that it was necessary to pacify and unify the country for the Constitution to have effect, particularly individual rights. He did not hesitate to use force to achieve his objective. He fought mercilessly against the supporters of Lerdo who were rebelling all over the country. At the same time he applied a conciliatory policy to this group which brought him more benefits than did armed struggle. For this he made an agreement with their leader, Matías Romero Rubio, and offered all his followers amnesty.

When this gray period ended there began to be a certain amount of uneasiness in society; while some people said that Díaz would stand for reelection, others flatly denied this. The general himself dispelled doubts by publicly stating that he would not run for reelection as this

General
Porfirio Díaz.

would be against what had been laid down in the Plan de Tuxtepec. The question then was who would be his successor. But this did not last long because from the beginning he showed support for his friend Manuel González, who ended being elected president of Mexico for the term 1880 - 1884 in an electoral process similar to those of Lerdo's times.

The task of Manuel González as president was to continue with the work begun by Díaz three years earlier, especially in the pacification of Mexico, and he managed to subdue the caciques of Puebla, Jalisco and Zacatecas. However, he made several mistakes and this, together with his lack of charisma, meant that he did not have popular support.

The most distrustful said that Díaz had not intervened to make González mend his ways, that on the contrary he had allowed him to act freely so that he and his followers would discredit themselves, True or not, the fact is that González governed so badly that many asked for Díaz to return. For this, changes would have to be made in the constitution for non-immediate reelection to be valid and in this way Díaz could occupy the presidency again.

When he took office for a second term (1884 - 1888), Díaz was a different man and politician. While González was president he took care to mold himself as a politician, as he was governor of Oaxaca between 1881 and 1883. He also married for the second time, to Carmen Romero Rubio, a young woman who helped him to improve himself and brought him into the world of society which although he did not like, he believed to be politically useful.

In this period, Díaz showed that he was prepared to use repression and antidemocratic practices as often as necessary if by this he succeeded in centralizing power and putting the country in order. He appointed the president and members of the Mexico City Ayuntamiento (municipal council) and the governors of several states, while he eliminated authorities and officials who opposed him, either politically or physically. He was also tough with the opposition press and imprisoned the journalists and editors who were most critical of him.

Díaz continued his campaign of pacification. He stepped up the fight against the individuals who were responsible for disorder and the banditry that was devastating the country, and forcefully put down Indian revolts (Mayas, Mayos and Yaquis).

Regional oligarchies were a danger because of the independence they showed to the central power. To subdue these groups, Díaz followed a dual policy, at first trying to buy their loyalty through granting privileges of all kinds, but as some refused to make any agreement he turned to violent repression as the only means of persuasion.

He also sought rapprochement with the Church because although he was a radical liberal, Juárez's experience had showed him that it was better to have it as an ally than an enemy. The political and religious authorities reached an agreement under which the Church would not interfere in matters of State, while this in turn would not concern itself with religious issues, and the more the clergy helped the government, the more tolerant it would be. Little by little the president controlled or subdued his potential enemies while he concentrated power in his person. It was not long before he brought all the important political authorities under his control.

By the end of this period, Porfirio Díaz had hardly begun to work on his projects and still had a lot to do. This is why Congress approved the plan to modify the Constitution put forward by the president where he proposed his immediate reelection for one term only. Díaz and his followers beat the opposition in elections.

It was in this period that the economy began to take off, but with great difficulty.

When Díaz took up office in 1877 he appointed Matías Romero Secretary of the Treasury. He was a politician whose greatest concerns were to balance the budget and solve the problem of public debt. He was able to do little in three years to find a solution to these issues and during the presidency of Manuel González (1880 - 1884), everything Romero had done collapsed because payments could not be made to foreign creditors and loans could not be sought from other countries. This is why it was decided to renegotiate the debt with England, which was a failure because the government recognized a debt higher than it held.

At this time, few rich countries were investing in Mexico because the country could not provide the necessary guarantees of political stability and social peace. To a certain extent this was a legacy from Maximilian's execution, which was seen in Europe as an act of barbarity produced by a lack of political order.

Between 1880 and 1884 the Mexican banking system began to be created. The Banco Nacional Mexicano was founded in 1881, thanks to the assistance of the Banque Franco-Égyptienne of Paris; a year later the Banco Mercantil, Agricola e Hipotecario with Spanish capital; the Banco Hipotecario and Banco de Empleados, both subsidiaries of the Banco de Londres y Mexico. Although the banking system was growing considerably, this was not enough to start up the domestic economy. From the beginning of his presidency, mining was a great concern for Díaz and therefore he tried, for the first time in history, to reorganize the industry to increase production and earn more income from exports. Clearly, in a times of tight liquidity, this goal was a difficult one to attain.

Like in the times of Juárez and Lerdo, during the Porfiriato it was thought that progress would come with the construction of railroads; this is why this means of transportation received great support but unfortunately could not be given shape due to lack of capital. At this period the question of large estates was not stressed. As this type of production was the only one which made agriculture a profitable business the regime encouraged their growth through Surveying Companies. These were responsible for measuring uncultivated lands and dividing them up for the government to sell later to individuals.

The Strengthening Process (1888 - 1904)

From the third reelection of Díaz there was such a continuity of ideas and plans that the general's administration can only be seen as unbroken —in 1890 he altered the Constitution to make continued reelection valid— and it would not be changed in any important way until the early 20th century.

The pacification process continued without problems because fewer and fewer groups and individuals were having recourse to revolt. However, the group that played a leading role in the most uprisings was that of the Indians who, as a result of the modernization of the country. were constantly being deprived of their land.

The decade of the nineties was the golden age of the Porfiriato as the president consolidated his power with the support of another group known as the *científicos* because of their belief that all the ills of humanity could be solved thorough science. The most outstanding were Francisco Buines, Ramón Corral, Enrique C. Creel, José Ives Limantour, Porfirio Parras, Justo Sierra, Emilio Rabasa, José López Portillo y Rojas, Joaquín Baranda and Diódoro Batalla, These men —who had no political power— became pillars of the country's economic growth since they controlled the banking system and acted as intermediaries between the government and Mexican and foreign investors.

By the middle of this decade Díaz was 60, which for the time was a considerable age The economic and political beneficiaries of the regime feared that the president's death was near and if action was not taken the country could fall back into the chaos that had been typical of it for so many years. The president was asked to agree to the creation of the post of vice-president, to fill it with someone he trusted and to prepare this person to succeed him. Diaz, suspicious that his vice-president might try to take away his power, flatly refused. He only allowed a few small changes in the Constitution so that if the president was absent his post would be occupied by the Secretary of Foreign Affairs or the Secretary of the Interior if the former post were empty or its holder unable.

The last four years of the 19th century saw great social unrest nationwide. For a start, society was tired of Díaz's dictatorship because despite the economic successes he had brought about, it could not endure the farce of elections every four years and people were clamoring for a real democracy, but no one dared to oppose the regime openly. Meanwhile, the Yaqui Indians (living in the state of Sonora) staged an armed revolt again in 1899 to prevent their lands and the use of the river Yaqui from being taken away for the benefit of the great estates, Their example was followed by Indians in Oaxaca, Veracuz and Yucatán.

Some politicians criticized the regime too. The conservatives branded Díaz as being a radical and criticized him for having imposed laicism, while the liberals accused him of having worked in collusion with conservative ideas and practices. These criticisms and demonstrations of discontent mattered little to the president because he was convinced that what he was doing was right for the good of the country.

In 1903, with the idea that he would need to govern for another term, Díaz accepted the position of vice-president; he realized that this was necessary so as to avoid problems if he died in office. In return he demanded that the presidential term of office be extended to six years, which the Porfirists gladly agreed to.

This was also a good time for the domestic economy. Although Díaz had worked to strengthen it since the previous period, it was now that its benefits could be felt fully at last. In 1888, Díaz's government began a policy to reduce government spending and increase taxes and exports to be able to pay off public debt and balance the budget. These aims were achieved in 1894 thanks to the part played by the Secretary of the Treasury, José Ives Limantour, a financial expert who achieved a surplus by reorganizing the Secretariat. With this surplus, the government was able to undertake more works of infrastructure in cities such as electric lighting. This financial success was partly due to the arrival of foreign capital in Mexico. News of Díaz's efforts to pacify and stabilize the nation spread all over the world and inspired enough confidence for foreign investors to gradually bring capital in.

The policy of surveying uncultivated land favored the creation of large Mexican and foreign estates which would become the basis of domestic agriculture and foster the growth of a land-owning aristocracy. Although there were some highly productive estates because they made good use of all the land, many estate owners farmed only a small part of their property and were content with producing what was necessary for them to maintain a high standard of living at the cost of the explotation of peasants, who worked from sunrise to sunset and lived in debt to company stores. These stores sold the peons basic goods and when they could not afford these, extended credit, as a result of which the peon was perpetually in debt. These debts were hereditary.

The End (1904 - 1911)

In contrast to the earlier years, from the first decade of the 19th century the government was concerned about repressing in any way possible the growing signs of discontent that different sectors of society were showing. The numbers of police in major cities were increased, new penitentiaries were opened such as on the Islas Marías and Lecumberri (today the National Archive) and local and regional authorities were given orders not to be tolerant of "subversive elements," in other words, to suppress them rapidly.

In spite of the above, the signs of unrest could not be quelled. An example of this was the strike movement at Cananea in 1906. As the company exploiting the mine was North American, the governor gave permission for a contingent of Arizona Rangers to intervene and supress the strikers. Some of the workers who took part in the strike were killed in the incursion while the survivors went back to work. The strike was backed by the Mexican Liberal Party which had been founded in 1902 by the brothers Enrique and Ricardo Flores Magón and others to put an end to the Díaz regime. The Party was persecuted and its members had to flee to the United States.

During these declining years of the Porfiriato an event occurred which seemed to brighten the panorama as it favored, though only in appearance, the peaceful transition to a new era. In 1908, President Díaz was interviewed by an American journalist by the name of Creelman. At one point Díaz spoke about the future of the country, in particular about the elections to be held in 1910. He stated that he would not seek reelection and looked favorably on the emergence of opposition parties, which was a clear acceptance of the birth of a democratic system in Mexico. This interview, seen as permission given by the dictator, eased the political atmosphere as middle and upper class groups began to found their own political parties, something they had never even imagined.

A year later, political parties were on the increase. The Democratic Party was founded, which had representatives of several political persuasions in its ranks. Its proposals were to restrict the vote to make it more effective, respect constitutional rights and create laws to protect workers and peasants.

Afraid of losing their privileges and position, in the middle of the year the Porfirists, without the president's consent, formed the Central Reelectionist Club, which at its national convention proposed Díaz as president and Ramón Corral vice-president for the period 1910 - 1916. In 1909, the Reyist Party was created which proposed Bernardo Reyes, the Secretary of War and governor of Nuevo León, as presidential candidate. This party included among its members a figure who was to become very important later: Venustianno Carranza. Reyist clubs, affiliates of the party, flourished all over the country to the extent that they were suppressed by the authorities.

Since the beginning of 1909 Francisco I. Madero, a hacienda owner from the state of Coahuila had been trying to organize a party under the banner *effective suffrage, no reelection,* In May he founded the Centro Anti-reeleccionista. Two members of the organization were José Vasconcelos and Luis Cabrera. Then Madero began touring the country with the idea of forming affiliated clubs which would attend a national convention on those candidates for the presidency and vice-presidency in the upcoming elections. The National Convention of the Centro Antireeleccionista was held in 1910, and there Madero was chosen as presidential candidate and the and the proposals of the party defined. These were no reelection of the president or vice-president, respect for the Constitution and all the rights it enshrined and the creation of decent living conditions for all Mexicans.

In 1910 society, and particularly the members of the Central Reelectionist Club, were astounded when Díaz accepted their invitation and made public his interest in being reelected. This changed the picture radically. Many people began to suspect that another fraud was being hatched while others, like Reyes, not wishing to have any trouble with the president, declined their candidature and consequently some political organizations had to be dismantled.

Madero did not become discouraged and went on with his proselytizing campaigns throughout Mexico. In July, 1910 he was in Monterrey and after finishing his speech he was thrown into prison along with his supporters on charges —fabricated— of sedition and offenses against authority. Later they were sent to the penitentiary in San Luis Potosí.

What motive did Díaz have for acting this way? It is a fact that Díaz wanted continuity in power and Madero was an obstacle to this. Some say that the only strong candidate that Díaz had to face in all his reelections was Madero, who was seen by the people as the only one strong enough to take the presidency from him.

Elections were held in July. Since Madero was in prison he could not compete in them and, as was to be expected, Díaz won again. When the danger was over, Madero and his companions were released while other members of his party unsuccessfully contested the electoral process in the House of Representatives. After this disastrous experience it became clear to Madero that the only way to bring about political and social change in the country was with arms.

Chapter 8

The Mexican Revolution: the Armed Struggle (1910 - 1917)

The Madero Stage (1910 - 1913)

Once free, Madero fled to San Antonio, Texas and there drew up the *Plan de San Luis Potosí* with some of his supporters, who included Aquiles Serdán. When Serdán returned to his hometown of Puebla he resisted an order of arrest in his in his house and was killed by the police, making him the first victim of the revolution. This document is traditionally considered the first of the Mexican Revolution, because it declared the elections null and void and the republic without leaders; Madero would assume the presidency provisionally and call for elections; he also promised Indians to return their lands and invited Mexicans to rise in arms on November 20, 1910.

When the day came, few rallied to the call to arms because the plan had hardly been made known and Madero had returned to Mexico the day before. The situation was different in early 1911 because several rebel groups had emerged in the north and center of the country. These movements were headed by men with different backgrounds and varying objectives. Pascual Orozco was a muleteer from a well-to-do family, who had not been able to fulfill his ambitions in Chihuahua because of the political and economic monopoly of the Terrazas clan. There was also Doroteo Arango, better known as Pancho Villa, devoted first and foremost to banditry. His actions had no ideological principles,

President
Francisco I.Madero.

rather they were gut reactions produced by the great resentment he felt against society. To attract men to his movement he proposed the allocation of land with the promise to make peasants smallholders.

One of the most famous leaders was Emiliano Zapata in the state of Morelos. He began the armed revolt so that the lands taken from the peasants would be returned to them and demanded land reform to benefit those who had never owned property. He proposed that the land returned be worked collectively. Although Zapata's work was praiseworthy, since he was one of the few peasants in Morelos who lived in decent circumstances, the problem of his movement was that it was very local.

Although these leaders, Madero himself included, had no military experience, they were able to organize armed contingents that time and again defeated an old, badly trained federal army with antiquated weapons. Although the generals hid these defeats from Díaz, he knew about them thanks to his spies, and in early 1911 they began to worry him.

When Ciudad Juárez fell into the hands of the revolutionaries (May, 1911) Medero was appointed provisional president and immediately began to make arrangements with Díaz for him to step down from power. Díaz knew that everything was lost and so agreed to negotiate with the rebels. At the end of the same month the two sides came to an agreement under which the president would resign on the condition Madero accepted Francisco León de la Barra (Secretary of Foreign Affairs) as interim president and promised not to make changes in the legislative and judicial powers. Although these conditions violated the Plan of San Luis Potosí, the revolutionary leader accepted them, considering that it was the only way to finalize the movement he had begun.

Díaz left the country for Europe on May 30. He never returned to Mexico and died in France, the man who had wielded absolute power in Mexico for nearly thirty years. Madero regarded the presidency of León de la Barra as a bridge between the fallen regime and the election of another. The demobilization of rebel troops was perhaps the most difficult task León de la Barra had to face because although his negotiations were successful in the north, in Morelos Emilano Zapata, leader of the Liberation Army of the South, made it clear that he would not hand over weapons until lands were returned to the peasants.

The presidential elections were held in late 1911 and were won by Madero and his running mate Pino Suárez. The climate was no longer favorable to the revolutionary leader as his agreement with Díaz, recognition of León de la Barra, and the fact that he had allowed the demobilization of the revolutionary troops had all taken away popularity and support. At the beginning, Madero's presidency was very difficult since both Congress and the Supreme Court were Porfirist and did their work very well, in other words they constantly opposed the president. Madero did not take any steps against this because he had agreed with Díaz that elections to remove these powers would be held in 1912 and he was prepared to keep his word.

Another factor which made Madero's political work difficult was the press. As a liberal, Madero removed the gags from the press so that it could operate with complete freedom of expression. Not even the warnings of his brother Gustavo A. Madero about the inadvisability of the press going from a state of complete submission to one of complete freedom dissuaded him from taking this step. With this freedom, the Porfirist press attacked him mercilessly. Naturally, the Maderist press went to the defense of the president but the use of rather dogmatic arguments, together with the suspicion that it was financed by the regime, robbed it of the power to convince.

One more problem in Madero's administration was the need to pacify the country. The president did not understand how it was possible there could be military leaders up in arms if the Revolution had fulfilled its objective —to topple Porfirio Díaz. What Madero did not understand was that each *caudillo* had a different idea of the Revolution and if for him it was to put and end to dictatorship, for Zapata, to give an example, it would not be over until land was divided and redistributed. Therefore, when Zapata, Orozco, Villa, Félix Díaz and others did not see their expectations met they continued to fight, only now against the new administration. One result was that in 1912 Zapata issued his *Plan de Ayala* and Orozco the *Pacto de la Empacadora*, documents which among other things repudiated Madero as legitimate president of Mexico.

Of all these movements, Madero considered that of the Zapatistas the most dangerous since it was spreading quickly in the area near Mexico City. At first Madero tried to hold talks with Zapata but they were not able to reach agreement since the president refused to carry out land redistribution. Following this, the president began armed pursuit of the revolutionary, which was a failure as he never managed to apprehend him.

Bernardo Reyes returned to Mexico in November 1911 to lead an uprising against Madero which would give him the presidency. He published the *Plan de la Soledad* in which he accused Madero of being a dictator, repudiated him as president of Mexico, and gave supreme command of the movement to the highest ranking officers. The plan was not followed by Mexican society and so Reyes was caught easily. Although according to law the prisoner should have been executed for treason, Madero commuted the sentence and had him imprisoned in

Emiliano Zapata.

the penitentiary of Santiago de Tlatelolco, Mexico City. In 1912 Pascual Orozco led another revolt against Madero's government and made public his *Pacto de la Empacadora*, a document which because it sought total support, was rather contradictory. In it Orozco repudiated Madero but strangely enough did not propose anyone as interim president. Orozco was the easiest of the rebel leaders to suppress; Madero sent General Victoriano Huerta to fight against him and he was captured in August 1912.

Another revolutionary leader was the nephew of Porfirio Díaz, Félix Díaz, who in October 1912 headed a rebellion against the government in the port city of Veracruz. He accused Madero of being unable to guarantee peace in the country. Federal troops defeated and took him prisoner easily. The Supreme Court, under pressure from the well-positioned groups in Mexico City, commuted his death sentence to life imprisonment. Like Bernardo Reyes, he was sent to the Tlatelolco penitentiary.

In actual fact, Madero was not able to do much for the country because his administration was more concerned with trying to solve political and military problems than governing. However, the real crisis came in February 1913.

On the ninth, a contingent led by General Manuel Mondragón made for the Tlatelolco prison to free Reyes and Díaz. As soon as Reyes was out he headed for the Plaza de la Ciudadela (formerly Mexico City's main square) to induce the National Palace garrison to rebel, but he was killed by bullets in the attack.

Félix Díaz and Mondragón established their headquarters in the Ciudadela, from where they intended to organize the president's fall. When Madero heard of this he went to the National Palace and ordered General Victoriano Huerta to force the entrenched rebels to yield. Huerta had his own plans and sent a representative to negotiate with them.

Meanwhile, the American ambassador in Mexico City, Henry Lane Wilson, decided to intervene in the conflict. On February 18 Díaz and Huerta a treaty with the ambassador as witness. In the Pact of the Embassy it was agreed that Huerta would arrest Madero and Pino Suárez and the presidency would be occupied temporarily for elections to be called, which it was agreed Félix Díaz would win. The following day, Huerta obliged Madero and Pino Suárez to tender their resignations to Congress, which named Pedro Lascuráin interim president. He named Huerta as the only member of his cabinet and resigned after 45 minutes. By elimination, Huerta was the next in line to occupy the presidency provisionally.. Madero and Pino Suárez were held prisoners in the National Palace and on February 22 they were shot outside the Mexico City prison to which they were being transferred.

The Administration of Victoriano Huerta (1913 - 1914)

Once in power and with Madero out of the way wanted his administration to be an extension of Porfirio Díaz's in ever sense. For this, had to put a peace campaign into motion which strangely enough did not begin with the use of weapons.

The pacification process also had its violent side as Huerta began a campaign against his opponents, having them assassinated in an example of the intolerance that was to prevail in his regime. When this campaign did not lessen the opposition of representatives and senators, Huerta decided to dissolve Congress and call elections to appoint a new, and of course more docile and loyal one. When the new Congress was elected in late 1913, many sworn followers of the president held places in both houses. This made Huerta's work easier because among other things he managed to break the agreement made with Félix Díaz by having Congress postpone the elections indefinitely.

Madero's death and the possibility of falling back into another dictatorship alarmed many revolutionaries, in particular Venustiano Carranza, the state governor of Chihuahua in the north. When Huerta came to power, he decided to organize a movement to unite all opponents to remove the usurper from the presidency, He named his movement "Constitutionalist," not because he wanted the country to have a new Constitution but because he wished the existing one —that of 1857— to be fully respected. To give this project more force he issued the *Plan de Guadalupe* which withdrew recognition of the three powers (executive, legislative and judicial), created the Constitutionalist army and provided that after victory, the leader of the movement (Carranza) would be appointed interim president and would call elections.

Carranza's great merit was that in a short time he was able to attract the major revolutionary leaders who also opposed Huerta to his cause (for example Obregón, Zapata, Villa and Benjamín Hill). He was also able to obtain support in the form of arms sales from the United States, a nation which did not recognize Huerta as the legitimate president of Mexico and looked favorably on the possibility of Carranza occupying the presidency.

This situation did not worry Huerta, particularly the support the revolutionaries were receiving from the United States, although nobody was selling his government war material, and he also thought that the

Francisco Villa.

marked disparity of personalities and plans among the members of the Constitutionalist army would prevent it triumphing.

Despite the large numbers of men he had, Huerta suffered a series of defeats all over the country against a revolutionary army which by mid 1914 controlled all the major cities. The president still held out the hope that the differences among the constitutionalists, especially between Francisco Villa and General Obregón would shatter the unity of the movement, but the timely intervention of Carranza to smooth over these differences prevented separation. A fundamental part of this work was the *Torreón Pact* which stipulated that on the movement's victory, a Convention would be installed made up of representatives of the Constitutionalist Army. This Convention would call general elections and draft a program of government.

The United States helped the rebels in yet another way. On April 21, 1913 it occupied the port of Veracruz, the nerve center of Mexican foreign trade, despite the valiant resistance put up by both the inhabitants and the cadets of the naval academy. On the pretext that some U.S. sailors had been mistreated in Tampico, ships and marines arrived in the port of Veracruz, occupied it and began to administer it. It was a hard blow for Huerta; he had finally managed to persuade Germany to sell him arms to fight his enemies but with the occupation of Veracruz they never reached him.

In Mexico City Huerta, in order to fight against the representatives of the opposition dissolved both houses and had the senator Belisario Domínguez and had two representatives —Serapio Rendón and Adolfo Gurrión— assassinated.

Unable to overcome the Constitutionalist armies, Huerta had no choice but to submit his resignation to Congress on July 15, 1914. Francisco Carbajal took his place as interim president, whose job it was to arrange for the revolutionaries to enter Mexico City.

The Struggle for Power amongst Revolutionaries (1914 - 1917)

After the dissolution of the federal army by the Treaty of Teoloyucan, State of Mexico, Carranza began having to face the differences that soon surfaced among the revolutionaries. Carranza's representatives were unable to persuade Zapata to be present at the Convention because he did not want it to be held in Mexico City. Villa took an ambiguous stance, sometimes saying that he would attend, and at other times threatening not to be present. This all came from his wish to annoy the Constitutionalist leader —with whom he had had several brushes over the last months. In fact he had no intention of going to the meeting.

The Convention began in Mexico City in October 1914, attended only by delegates who supported Carranza. He was recognized as interim president and also it was debated about whether it would be better to move the Convention to the town of Aguascalientes so that Villa's representatives would attend, and the proposal was accepted. When Villa learned of this he agreed to send delegates and shortly afterward Zapata yielded too.

Aguascalientes was controlled by the Villist army, and so was a danger for Carranza who, having seen how Villists and Zapatists formed a united front against him decided to go to Veracruz and avoid the Convention because he knew that there, all was lost. This did not prevent the delegates at the Convention from electing Eulalio Gutiérrez provisional president for a period of 20 days. Carranza refused to recognize the election because Gutiérrez was a staunch supporter of Villa. The reply that the Zapatists and Villists gave him was simple and flat: they agreed to move the Convention to Mexico City whenever Villa should enter.

By December 1915, tension was running so high among the revolutionaries that everything seemed to indicate there would be an armed conflict between them. Carranza made some changes to his *Plan de Guadalupe* so as to win more supporters. The additions were of a social nature including land reform, improving the living standards of laborers and peasants and establishing a fairer system.

Villa and his men marched to Mexico City with the president. Unruliness and abuses were the order of the day and the inhabitants of the city could witness that the one who governed was Villa, not Gutiérrez.

In early 1915, the armed struggle between Villa and Zapata against Carranza broke out. After the first encounters, Villism spread through the north and west of the country while Carranza concentrated his efforts on taking back the capital, which was achieved on January 28, 1915, when General Alvaro Obregón's army defeated Zapata's supporters who held the city, with the result that the Convention moved to Cuernavaca. This event helped to terminate the alliance between Villa and Zapata, since for the former, the second was no longer important from a military point of view.

Obregón then began a systematic campaign against Villa. On April 6 and 7 he was able to defeat him in the Bajío region in the two battles of Celaya, where Villa realized that he was finished militarily. Therefore he wanted to ingratiate himself with Carranza, but he refused and ordered Obregón to continue his campaign. In the attack Obregón made on Celaya he lost his right arm as a result of a grenade wound.

Villa, in retreat in the north, devoted himself to constant guerilla action, and wishing to complicate things internationally for Carranza and at the same time take revenge on the Americans for not recognizing his government, attacked the town of Columbus (New Mexico) with groups of cavalry The U.S. government sent troops under General John Pershing into Mexico on a punitive expedition. The Americans searched a large part of Chihuahua but never found Villa.

With Francisco Villa militarily weakened and Emiliano Zapata besieged in the state of Morelos, Carranza decided that the time had come to convoke a constituent Congress to give the country a new Constitution. This change of opinion was due to the fact that the Revolution had led to so many changes in Mexico that it was impossible for it to continue being governed by a Constitution that had been created in another context and era.

The Congress began meeting in Querétaro in December, 1916. Neither Zapatists nor Villists were included, since Carranza wanted only the "victors" of the Revolution to take part. Despite this, two trends emerged: the moderates, who held the orthodox liberal ideology, and the radicals, who proposed the creation of a strong State which would promote social reforms. The debates between the two factions were very fruitful since they usually ended in jointly made proposals, which in turn made it possible to promulgate a Constitution on February 5, 1917, the most advanced of its time, and containing anticlerical articles.

Chapter 9

Creation and Consolidation of the Revolutionary State (1917 - 1940)

The Presidency of Venustiano Carranza's (1917 - 1920)

Elections were held in March, 1917 to renew the executive and legislative powers. Venustiano Carranza was elected president of the country and his candidates obtained all the seats in the House of Representatives and the Senate.

When Carranza assumed the presidency he had to resort to some of the tactics used by Díaz decades earlier. Like the dictator, the president realized that the centralization of power in the hands of the executive went hand in hand with this process. For this reason, he ordered the congresses of each state in the republic to call elections for the renovation of powers. The results of the elections were favorable for the president since almost all the Carrancist candidates were able to occupy the disputed governorships.

As this was still an epoch in which "rough Mexico" was near the surface, he knew that not all the malcontents and armed rebels would collaborate voluntarily. Since it was a fact that there would be the need to repress them so as to bring order to the country it was important to have a loyal and efficient army up to the task, but the Mexican army

Venustiano
Carranza.

that had emerged during the Revolution had neither of these qualities, and therefore would have to be reshaped.

The overhaul had very little success because lack of sufficient funds precluded the application of a plan for early retirement and the hiring of good teachers for military academies. In addition, the Revolution had left so many bad habits in the army that they could not be eradicated in the short term, only with reforms to be made over time. Despite this, the army that had emerged from the Revolution partly fulfilled the task and in the space of three years it succeeded in subduing and executing Emiliano Zapata and generals Felipe Ángeles and Manuel Blanquet, all important revolutionaries. Perhaps the most sensational was Zapata's because his death was due to a betrayal thought up by the government. It arranged an ambush on the hacienda of Chinameca, Morelos, in which Zapata was killed on April 10, 1919.

The Congress was a headache for Carranza, because the break between him and General Obregón (largely caused by the political ambitions of the latter) was not open and public, the representatives and senators were loyal to him. However, when appearances could be kept up no longer, the members of the legislative demonstrated their support of Obregón as a younger and more charismatic leader.

The economy became a great worry for Carranza because the Revolution had destroyed the system created during the Porfiriato and plunged the country into crisis. To stabilize the currency the president ordered it to be backed by gold, giving the pesos a value of 75 centigrams of precious metal because this was the only way to revalue the peso against the dollar. The first Congress of Industrialists was organized, where the needs of domestic industry were discussed. An attempt was made to rebuild the railroad network, which had been devastated in the upheaval (revolutionaries would blow up tracks to derail trains carrying federal troops), but it could not be done because there were no funds available.

The famous *Zimmerman Telegram* had reached the president in 1917. This was an invitation from the German foreign minister for Mexico to break its neutrality in the First World War and take Germany's side. In return, Germany promised to return Texas and the other territory lost to the United States in 1848. It was a very inviting offer, but Carranza decided that what it proposed was very a very risky prospect and so turned it down.

One way to end the armed stage of the Revolution and provide different, legitimate spaces for the people to express their disagreements with the government and at the same time help to strengthen the country in is politics were the parties. Those first to surface from the Revolution were small groups adhered to local leaders; there were very few real parties spanning the nation.

Undeniably, political parties are linked to the question of elections. In 1919 Mexicans began to think about the elections to be held the following year because they would be the first post-Revolution ones. After the convocation was made public, the first to stand for the presidency was General Álvaro Obregón.

Obregón had quietly begun his electoral campaign in 1917 and now seized the opportunity to bring his effort to fruition. From the beginning he did not hesitate to criticize Carranza, his old chief, companion in arms and friend as immoral and incapable of pacifying the country. The president replied to these attacks by nominating a friend of his for the residency to hinder his enemy. The problem was that his candidate, Ignacio Bonilla, was an unknown and, for many people, a puppet of the president.

A serious reversal for the president was when the army began to show its support for Obregón. Proclamations and manifestos to this effect were published daily in newspapers or were affixed to posts and doors in major cities. The situation grew worse when the governor of Sonora, Adolfo de la Huerta, a close friend of Obregón's, proclaimed the *Plan de Agua Prieta* in 1920 which repudiated Carranza as president and proposed that once the government had been brought down a general election should be called.

The uprising throughout the country was supported by both the army and civilians, which was enough to make Carranza decide to leave the capital and make for Veracruz from where he would set about "reconquering" power. But this was not to be. On May 20 the president and some of his men reached the village of Tlaxcalantongo in the mountains of Puebla on horseback and decided to spend the night in some huts there. At three o'clock in the morning of the next day several men attacked the shack where Carranza was sleeping and assassinated him.

The interim Presidency of Adolfo de la Huerta (1920)

When news of the fateful incident became public Congress elected Adolfo de la Huerta provisional president.

Although the reason behind De la Huerta's presidency was to pave the way for Obregón to win the election he did work to pacify the country.

He reduced the army from 200,000 men to only 50,000; those who were demobilized were given land and brought together in army colonies or else employed as workers in government factories.

He also fought against revolutionaries who had still not laid down their arms. In this, de la Huerta gained fame by obtaining the surrender of Francisco Villa who after waging guerilla warfare since 1916 gave himself up to the federal government in return for a hacienda in Chihuahua by the name of *Canutillo*. Some time later, he was assassinated in his car together with a few of his followers when on a visit to the nearby town of Parral.

As had been agreed at the beginning of his term, de la Huerta called elections for September. 1920. Alvaro Obregón was the outright winner, with 95% of the votes in an election rigged to favor him over the other candidates;

The Presidency of Alvaro Obregón (1920 - 1924)

When Obregón became president his objective was to give continuity, although it may seem a contradiction, to Carranza's work to create a strong State based on the ideals of the Revolution. To achieve this end he believed it was necessary to fight all obstacles, particularly regional political control (i.e. local political leaders) impeding the centralization of power.

But things were not easy for Obregón, especially because of the problems he had with the United States. The U.S. government refused to recognize him as legitimate president because he had supposedly been a party to the revolt which ended with the assassination of Victoriano Carranza. In 1920 and 1921 informal talks were held between the two nations which did not lead to any agreement. The matter was taken up again in 1923 and for this a mixed commission was set up and three months later the Bucareli Agreements were signed in which recognition of the Obregón administration and future governments of Mexico were made conditional on that:

1.- The Mexican government would pledge to compensate American citizens resident in the country for damage suffered between 1862 and 1917.

2.- Article 27 of the Constitution would not be retroactive, i.e. Americans who had acquired mines, oil wells or other property before February 5, 1917 would not be affected by the Mexican Constitution.

To concentrate power, the president decided to seek the aid of the army which was becoming more loyal to the government day by day. The use of troops to subdue local political bosses in opposition to the federal government was an effective method used by Obregón to concentrate power; they were either repressed or pursued by the army.

He also made an effort to have more control over the workers' movement and for this made structural improvements to its organizations. Obregón gave all his encouragement to the workers affiliated to the CROM (Confederación Regional Obrera Mexicana) and in return was given its complete support. The independent workers' organizations were the ones which gave the government most trouble with their rebellious attitude. For the authorities, union unrest was dangerous because it worked against the centralization of power.

As a rancher from the north, the president wanted to create small property owners so that farmers would feel responsible for their land and increase productivity. Most peasants wanted the opposite however: community land where the lack of tools would be made up for by an abundant supply of manpower. The clamor was so strong that the president had to yield and distribute land in the form of communal property *(ejidos)*. Thanks to this, Obregón enjoyed the unconditional support of peasant farmers all through his administration.

The president had sufficient vision to realize that one way to spread the ideals of the Revolution and create a nationalism based on its ideas, was education. This important task was given to José Vasconcelos, the first Secretary of Education in Mexico, who began a nationwide literacy campaign. Diego Rivera, José Clemente Orozco and David Alfaro

Siqueiros were commissioned to paint murals on public buildings (mainly government ones) with colossal images embodying the ideals of the revolution enshrined with a socialist ideology based on the recovery of the indigenous heritage and the government's social work. Thus was the later to be famous "Mexican muralism" born.

As had happened years earlier, the presidential succession was not peaceful and resulted in an internal dispute among the group of revolutionaries. In 1923, the names circulating as successors to the president were Adolfo de la Huerta, Secretary of the Treasury and Plutarco Elías Calles, Secretary of the Interior. The rumors were well founded since both were close friends of the president and backed by politically strong groups.

On several occasions de la Huerta stated publicly that he had no intention of taking part in he elections because he knew that Calles had Obregón's support. When Calles's bid for president became public, many career army officers were against him because Calles, apart from not having much charisma, had the reputation of being very strict and demanding. Therefore, they began pressing de la Huerta to stand; he resigned from the Ministry of the Interior but did not make his aspirations known. Obregón did not want this politician to spoil his plans and so had him accused of misappropriation of funds during his tenure as Secretary of the Treasury, to which de la Huerta responded by agreeing to stand for president.

As he knew that he was not going to win cleanly because it was against the president's wishes, de la Huerta went to Veracruz and there rose up in armed revolt against the government. He accused the president of violating the sovereignty of states, repressing the legislative power, trying to assassinate representatives and wanting to continue governing the country through Calles. The Huertist movement took root all over the country but Obregón waged a successful military campaign against the rebels, taking advantage of the disorganization that reigned among them. When the uprising was quelled the leaders who were not able to escape to the United States were executed before a firing squad, with the exception of Adolfo de la Huerta whose life was pardoned because he had been president, on the condition that he leave the country.

Once all this was over, elections were held in July 1924 which carried General Plutarco Elías Calles to the presidency for the term 1924 - 1928.

The Presidency of Plutarco Elías Calles (1924 - 1928)

Calles continued the project of the revolutionary State left to him by Obregón. He thought the ever stronger centralizing role of the State should have greater influence on society as a whole.

Calles recognized the importance of the army reforms carried out by his predecessors, but believed that after what had happened in the Huerta revolt it was necessary to reform the organization to make it more loyal to the president. He charged the secretary of War, General Joaquin Amaro with the job. Amaro implemented a program of modernization that was very effective. He reopened the Military Academy which had been closed since 1914, designed a program to make officers professionals, expelled those suspected of being likely to organize armed rebellions and as a final step divided the country into 33 military zones and ordered the heads of them to be rotated every six months to prevent personal alliances and loyalties toward other officers.

Neither politicians, workers nor peasants or the U.S. government presented the greatest obstacle against the strengthening of the revolutionary state. Although the story might seem hackneyed and old, it was again the Church that interfered in state plans. Ever since Carranza's administration, relations between the two had not been good, essentially because the Church refused to accept the *Constitution of 1917* because of its frankly anticlerical nature. However, both Carranza and Obregón, despite their avowed atheism, took care not to antagonize the clergy.

But all this changed with Calles because from 1927 to 1929 there was a bloody rebellion which went down in Mexican history as the Cristero rebellion or *Cristera* located mainly in the Bajío region, Michoacán, Jalisco, Colima, parts of Zacatecas, Durango, Guerrero and Oaxaca. The Cristeros were those who fought against the State in defense of the Church and their religious convictions.

In face of this aggression against the Church, a considerable group of laymen founded the *National League for Religious* Freedom to stop it and demand the government to respect the freedom of worship enshrined in the Constitution. Its members asked for the government not to have the power to legislate in religious affairs and for all the articles that went against the free practice of Catholicism to be repealed. At the same time, the episcopate (i.e. all the bishops and archbishops of the country) created "The Committee," an organism designed to communicate with the government in everything concerning the modification of the laws which submitted the Church to the will of the State.

The Cristero war began already bogged down, with neither army winning or losing positions. At the beginning this movement seemed madness because it was thought that the federal army, being made up of professional soldiers and possessing better equipment, would soon defeat the rebels, who were an improvised band. In fact, the Cristeros made up for these deficiencies with courage and tight union, knowledge of the land and the support of the population. It was common to see rich and poor, landowners and peons, entrepreneurs and workers, laymen and priests in the ranks, all united in the cause.

In face of this stalemate, in 1928 there began to be a moderate stance in the episcopate showing an interest in seeking rapprochement with the government to end the bloody fighting. The president, who was in his last days of office, also wanted to put an end to the situation but as he did not want to make direct contact with the religious authorities, he decided to find a mediator acceptable to both parties. This could not be done however as Calles's presidency terminated on December 1, 1928.

One very important economic aspect of the Calles administration was the countryside. He saw that the agricultural problem was technological and not restricted simply to land distribution. It was his ambition to create a large class of small landowners, but at the same time he was not against communal lands *(ejidos)* because they were an ideal way of suppressing large estates. The government's concern about the agrarian question led to many laws being passed which protected the members of cooperatives and their land from possible abuses by local authorities and obliged the government to provide them with irrigation systems.

Calles's oil policy was openly nationalistic and can be considered a forerunner of the expropriation. In 1927 he passed the Petroleum Law under which the foreign oil companies had to negotiate a 50-year permit with the Mexican government to exploit wells acquired before May 1, 1917. Any companies which did not agree to this ruling would lose their rights over wells. The Calles administration had to retreat because of pressure from the American government which came to the defense of its oil companies.

The election of 1928 was one of the most interesting in Mexican 20th century history because it shook one of the basic revolutionary principles: the non reelection of the president.

During the Calles administration, Obregón had apparently retired from politics and was busy with agriculture, although he was confident he would soon return to the political scene. This confidence arose from an oral agreement he had made with Calles in 1923 to the effect that the two would alternate in the presidency, four years one then four years the other. In late 1927, when Calles still had not made known his candidate, Obregón began to put pressure on him to alter Article 82 of the Constitution to make non-immediate reelection legal. Calles was loath to do this because he had the idea that once Obregón returned to power he would not keep his word. But his friend's pressure was so strong that in 1928 he made Congress alter the Article.

Many politicians did not accept the change, especially those who aspired to the office of president, as being a violation of the Constitution of 1917. Therefore, Generals Francisco Serrano, and Arnulfo R. Gómez

144

rebelled against Calles and Obregón and stood as opposition candidates. The president did not want this problem to grow and so had Serrano arrested and killed in the village of Huitzilac, Morelos, and his body taken to Mexico City. Three days later General Gómez and some of his followers were captured and shot in Veracruz.

The Catholics also tried to oppose this project. A bomb was thrown at Obregón's automobile from a moving car in Chapultepec park. Although the candidate was not injured, Mexico City authorities carried out an investigation which revealed that those responsible were Luis Segura Vilchis, Humberto Pro Juárez and the Jesuit Miguel Agustín Pro, all members of the National League for Religious Freedom. They were arrested and executed.

On July 2, 1928, Obregón won at the polls and became president-elect. However, as he was celebrating his victory in La Bombilla park 15 days later he was shot by the artist León Toral. He turned out to be a religious fanatic who had been persuaded by the abbess Concepción Acevedo to commit the crime. The perpetrator of the assassination and the author of the plan were tried and sentenced, Toral to death and the abbess to 20 years imprisonment. The radical Obregonists, despite all the evidence, accused Calles of masterminding the murder. Calles defended himself saying that it was the first time in years that the country had no caudillos and this favored the step from a Mexico of caudillos to a Mexico of political institutions; from then on the press called him "the Supreme Chief (Jefe Máximo) of the Mexican Revolution."

The Maximato (1928 - 1934)

The name Maximato is given to the period in which Mexican politics were controlled by the Jefe Máximo of the Revolution: Plutarco Elías Calles. Since Calles could not occupy the presidency in the period immediately following his own term of office, and did not want reelection because of what had happened after Obregón's assassination, he thought it would be better to govern the country by manipulating presidents imposed discreetly by him.

Because of the surprise caused by the assassination, Calles had to find an interim president. He chose Emilio Portes Gil for several reasons: he was not linked to either Obregón's cause or that of Calles and moreover was an eminent politician.

Portes Gil understood his position from the very beginning. Proof of this was his interest, because he devoted himself to the Calles project of consolidating the revolutionary State and developing Mexico's economy. By virtue of this, he supported Calles when he began to organize a new political party that was to unite and bring discipline to all the revolutionary family. December 1928 saw the formation of the National Revolutionary Party (PNR) —which was the first name of the present Institutional Revolutionary Party (PRI). The Supreme Chief was appointed its leader and ordered all public officials to join. The party also represented, and at the same time wanted to control, the bases of Mexican society, that is to say workers and rural workers who together made up the greater part of the population.

Another major event was the Escobar rebellion. In March 1929 an armed revolt broke out in various states led by Gonzalo Escobar. Under the banner of the *Plan of Hermosillo*, the rebels withdrew recognition from Portes Gil as president and from all the authorities who did not support the movement and tat the same time invited the populace to second their protest. Faced with this prospect, the president appointed Calles secretary of War and the Navy so that he could halt the rebels. This he succeeded in doing three months later by capturing and shooting the rebels or sending them into exile.

In religious affairs Portes Gil, counseled by Calles, solved the Cristero conflict. In 1929, the Church and State agreed that Dwight Morrow, the U.S. ambassador should be the mediator. It was thanks to his steps that an accord was reached known as the Agreements of 1920 under which the Church pledged not to interfere in politics, in return for which the State would endeavor to be more tolerant in the application of religious legislation. In fact, the two parties agreed that the situation should remain what it was before the fighting broke out. Many Cristeros and government supporters were annoyed at this because they and their families had made great sacrifices, only to see that in the end things did not change.

Political agitation began in late 1929; speculations as to who the "official" candidate for president would be circulated throughout the country. In the opinion of many people, the man who stood the best chance was Aaron Sáenz, the governor of Nuevo León, because he was a friend of Calles's and skilled in government. Actually, this was his greatest defect because Calles thought that once in the presidency he would show rebelliousness and refuse to be manipulated. So he recalled Pascual Ortiz Rubio to Mexico to stand as the presidential candidate of the PNR. Rubio considered the invitation just, thinking that only now were his merits as a revolutionary being recognized. But the truth of the matter was different. The diplomat did not know what was happening in Mexico and did not have a political party behind him for support. In March, 1929, during the First National Convention of the PNR, the base members of the party elected Pascual Ortiz Rubio as their candidate for the presidency 1930 - 1934.

When everything seemed ready for the Calles candidate's victory, there appeared José Vasconcelos, the former secretary of Education. He was the strongest opponent of the official candidate since he had managed to gather together most of the 1910 revolutionaries and the anti-government opposition from the National Anti-Reelectionist party.

The Vasconcelos campaign began in the United States and quickly spread to Mexico, where it had some setbacks (cases of unjustified imprisonment, the disappearance of followers...) most of them planned by the government. This caused the candidate to think that there would be an election fraud in favor of Ortiz Rubio. After elections in which fraud was a constant, Pascual Ortiz Rubio was declared president elect of Mexico for the period 1930 - 1934. José Vasconcelos felt cheated but with no other options left to him he went into self-imposed exile in the United States and never returned to Mexico.

The administration of Ortiz Rubio issued the Estrada Doctrine which still defines Mexico's position with regard to recognizing the governments of other countries. The principle of this document is non-intervention in the domestic affairs of any nation.

There was a crisis in late 1931 when Calles made Ortiz Rubio ask for the resignation of four army officers in the cabinet (including Joaquín Amaro and Lázaro Cárdenas) despite the fact that the president had invited them to work with him a short time before. Calles gave Ortiz Rubio the coup de grace when he appointed himself secretary of War and the Navy. This obliged the president to submit his resignation on September 2, 1932, with the explanation that by doing so he was avoiding discord among the revolutionaries and that in addition his health prevented him from continuing in office,

After his resignation the House of Representatives met again to designate an interim president who would be acceptable to Calles. Finally they chose Abelardo Rodríguez because he lacked the support of any particular political group, which to a large extent would make relations with the Supreme Chief easier during the interim president's term of office. From the beginning it was made clear to Rodríguez that he would be a kind of administrator responsible for implementing the measures and provisions planned by Calles.

The presidency of Rodríguez elapsed in an atmosphere rarified by the general concern to know who the next president would be. Manuel Pérez Treviño, Carlos Riva Palacio and Lázaro Cárdenas were the names most mentioned. The last on the list, an army officer from Michoacán who carried a lot of political weight was chosen by Calles as the PNR presidential candidate. After being nominated Cárdenas pursued a campaign all over the country which ranged from major cities to the most isolated hamlets.

The Administration of Lázaro Cárdenas (1934 - 1940)

At the beginning of Cárdenas's term of office, people did not place many expectation in him because they thought that he too would be controlled by Calles. Circumstances seemed to indicate this because when Cárdenas took the presidency, his cabinet had been created by the *Supreme Chief* and contained mostly Calles supporters; the representatives and senators, state governors and heads of military zones were all loyal to Calles.

At the beginning the president took certain measures designed to win popular support. He reduced his salary by half, changed the presidential residence from Chapultepec Castle to Los Pinos —which he had had built— because he thought the castle was too luxurious and ordered Telegraphs of Mexico not to charge people who wanted to send a telegram to the presidency. Although these measures might be seen as populist today, at the time they earned much support for Cárdenas, because ever since the campaign people had seen him as an approachable man who really cared about their problems.

With the people behind him, Cárdenas very soon began to give signs that he wanted to be independent. He had dishonest businesses run by Callists closed; replaced the chiefs of military operations, stepped up land redistribution and supported the workers, allowing them to exercise their right to strike more freely.

This was when Calles decided that a good way to lessen Cárdenas's impetus was to attack him in the press. In June 1935 an interview was published in all Mexico City's newspapers in which Calles criticized the labor policy of the moment, asserting that strikes damaged the country because they were frightening foreign capital and as a result sources of employment for workers were being closed. Cárdenas reacted by asking for the resignation of all his cabinet, demanding the loyalty of the new chiefs of military zones and eliminating Callists from Congress, state governorships and the PNR.

The *Supreme Chief* was furious at Cárdenas's insolence and opted to leave for the United States on June 18 the same year to let the situation calm down. He returned in December only to find a stronger Cárdenas and an atmosphere that was against him and therefore continued his attacks on labor policy and the Cardenas administration. By this time the president had enough power and popular support to take a decisive step: he ordered Calles expelled from the country on April 10, 1936. With this decree Cárdenas put an end to the Maximato and enabled Mexico to become a country of institutions.

In 1936 the Union of Oil Workers of Mexico was formed, and a year later it helped oil workers to go on strike. They demanded an increase in wages with more benefits, and collective agreements. While the oil companies said they agreed to the second demand, they said they could not yield to the first because their profit margin was very narrow. Since bosses and workers were unable to reach agreement the dispute was taken before the Federal Labor Commission, which found in favor of the workers. The well owners did not accept the decision and turned to the Supreme Court to contest the verdict, but the judicial power rejected the appeal as being without legal grounds and ordered the companies to meet the demands of the workers. The owners of the oil companies refused to comply and began to counter the workers by hiring strikebreakers. Cárdenas decided to intervene and on March 18, 1938 decreed the nationalization of the oil companies in a step that ensured the country of recovering control of its most important natural resource.

The changes made by Cárdenas were so large and controversial that by 1938 that Mexicans were divided about the president. There were those who had benefited from his policies (workers and peasants) and those who saw their economic and social interests adversely affected (upper classes and great landowners). This discontent was channeled, at least on one occasion, in a revolt led by Saturnino Cedillo, the political boss of San Luis Potosí. Although his banner was that to remedy the excesses committed by the president, his real motivation was to reach power through the force of arms because he knew very well that his friendship with Cárdenas was not going to make him nominate him presidential candidate for the 1940 elections, Faced with the rebellion, Cárdenas showed himself vigorous and sent a contingent of troops and state peasants to quell the uprising. In under two months, Cedillo was executed and his movement stamped out.

Despite his victory, Cárdenas understood that this episode had been caused by the tension prevailing in the country and that although he was at the end of his term of office, he could prevent things becoming worse when it was time to choose his successor. After weighing things up he decided to choose a man of the center who could pacify the situation and reinforce some of the achievements of his presidency. The man was Manuel Ávila Camacho, an army officer different from other presidents because he had not played a very outstanding role in the armed stage of the Revolution.

Nine presidents of the PRI followed General Ávila Camacho. Miguel Alemán, from 1946 to 1952; Adolfo Ruiz Cortines from 1952 to 1958; Adolfo López Mateos, 1958 to 1964; Gustavo Díaz Ordaz from 1964 to 1970; Luis Echeverría, 1970 to 1976; José López Portillo, 1976 to 1982; Miguel de la Madrid from 1982 to 1988; Carlos Salinas de Gortari, 1988 to 1994 and Ernesto Zedillo from 1994 to 2000 and two who came from the ranks of the National Action Party (PAN): Vicente Fox Quesada from 2000 to 2006 and Felipe Calderón Hinojosa, who took office on December 1, 2006."

Epilogue

This is how our trip through Mexico's past end, but not its history.

After Cárdenas stepped down from power, regimes decided to make some changes to the operation of the revolutionary State.

Little by little, rural areas lost importance for the government because the peasants stopped being Mexico's largest social group, yielding this place to workers. Industrialization became the main target in the nation's development, although this led to closer diplomatic and economic ties to the United States which have become stronger since the Free Trade Agreement was signed in the nineties.

As the party (since 1946 called the Partido Revolucionario Institucional or PRI) acquired power and grouped together more sectors of society, the country entered a period of political and social calm, although it was not free from problems.

On December 1, 2000 the country experienced an important change since the opposition came to power, with Vicente Fox Quesada as president, after the revolutionaries and their ideological heirs had governed for 83 years. The PAN continues in power since the new president, Felipe Calderón, also belongs to the same party."

Printed in:
Programas Educativos, S.A. de C.V.
Calz. Chabacano No. 65 Local A
Col. Asturias
06850 - México, D.F., April 2007
Empresa Certificada por el ISO-9002